Thanks for the glorious —
unforgettable tour of
another part of our great
Montana land. ...... There are
no words for the beauty
even at 160 MPH 2R I style!

I love you ~
SB&O
July 1690

CORVETTE

SPORTS CAR ~ SUPERCAR

CORVETTE

SPORTS CAR ~ SUPERCAR

TERRY JACKSON

COURAGE
BOOKS

An imprint of
RUNNING PRESS
PHILADELPHIA, PENNSYLVANIA

A QUINTET BOOK

Text copyright © 1990
Quintet Publishing Limited

First published in the United States of
America in 1990 by Courage Books, an
imprint of Running Press Book Publishers.

9 8 7 6 5 4 3 2 1
Digit on the right indicates the number of
this printing.

Library of Congress Cataloguing-in-
Publication Number 89-81979

ISBN 0-89471-830-4

This book was designed and produced by
Quintet Publishing Limited
6 Blundell Street
London N7 9BH

Creative Director: Peter Bridgewater
Designer: James Lawrence
Editor: Shaun Barrington
Archive Picture Researcher: Julie Wright

Typeset in Great Britain by Central Southern
Typesetters, Eastbourne.
Manufactured in Hong Kong by Regent
Publishing Services Limited.
Printed in Hong Kong by Lee Fung Asco
Printers Limited.

This book may be ordered by mail from the
publisher. Please add $2.50 for postage and
handling for each copy. But try your
bookstore first.
Running Press Book Publishers
125 South Twenty-second Street
Philadelphia, Pennsylvania 19103

CONTENTS

An American icon   6

A dream becomes a reality   10

Zora to the rescue   22

Corvette goes racing . . . sort of   34

From sports car to muscular dragster   48

The enduring Sting Ray   58

Corvettes that never were   78

The Corvette returns to the winner's circle   96

At last, a world class Corvette   102

Index   126

AN AMERICAN ICON

The boy brought his bicycle to a dead stop on the sidewalk outside the suburban California shopping mall. He deftly balanced the 10-speed racing cycle with one foot on the ground and the other in the pedal stirrup. He was gazing with rapt attention at a car, oblivious to the ebb and flow of shoppers around him. In his eyes was a longing and admiration that shines particularly clearly on the face of a youth in his early teens.

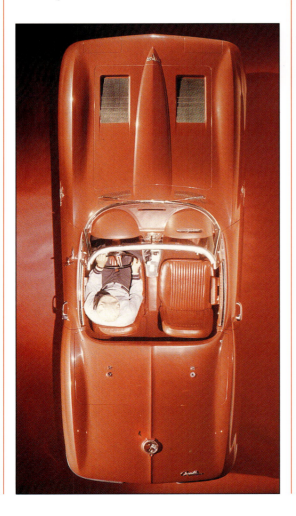

ABOVE 1955 : a mere 700 units were sold. Only the determination of a handful of managers, designers and engineers with faith in the Corvette saved it from premature death.

RIGHT The 1984 Corvette; the first radically different Corvette design for 15 years.

LEFT Bill Mitchell's Sting Ray, a classic car of the 1960s, and now the most collectible Corvette on the market.

The object of his desire was a yellow 1990 Corvette convertible, left parked at the curb while the owner dashed inside one of the mall shops. The top down, the saddle-tan leather seats soaking up the late summer sun, the Corvette looked like a golden sword just pulled from its scabbard.

Slowly, the boy walked his bicycle toward the Corvette, his eyes sweeping over every line. He took in the huge 17-inch Goodyear tires, the steeply raked windshield, the clean rear deck lines. Urging the bike forward, the boy moved off the sidewalk and onto the asphalt parking lot, gently circumnavigating the Corvette. He stopped at the rear and bent over to inspect the dual quad exhaust pipes, then proceeded on, looking into the interior and finishing up at the nose.

Just then the owner, a man in his late 30s, returned to his Corvette. As he opened the driver's door and slipped into the bucket seat, he and the boy exchanged smiling glances. The driver's expression said he could recall when he was a boy on the bike lusting after a Corvette. The boy's face said that one day he would be the man behind the wheel of a Corvette.

The scene is one that an advertising executive would give his corner office to capture, one suitable for a Norman Rockwell painting. And yet it is a commonplace scene where the Corvette is concerned.

In car-crazy America, no automobile has inspired the huge admiration and almost cultlike following linked to the Corvette. For close on 40 years the Corvette has been an icon of American pop culture, a car that many aspire to own or, for even a brief moment, drive.

'The Corvette has always looked exciting when compared to other American cars,' says *Automobile* columnist Bob Cumberford. 'It has always been by far the sportiest American car, even for the three years when the Thunderbird was a two-seater.'

When it was introduced in 1953, it was the darling of movie stars and captains of industry. John Wayne owned one of the first Corvettes, although it is rumored he was too tall to comfortably drive it. In later years the car was the featured player in the television

ABOVE *The amazing Corvette Indy prototype, first revealed in 1986, teasingly described by Chevy as "an early look at a project under development."*

show 'Route 66'. It's doubtful America's television audience would have cared nearly as much about the adventures of Todd and Buzz if they'd toured Route 66 in a Nash.

When the quest for outer space gripped America, and its heroes were seven hot test pilots called the Mercury Astronauts, the Corvette was there. Through an arrangement with a Florida Chevrolet dealer, all of the astronauts had new Corvettes each year so they could fly low on the highways when they weren't circling the earth.

In the Jan and Dean surf-sound rock 'n' roll hit 'Deadman's Curve', it's a Corvette that carries the day in the refrain' all the Jag could see was my six tail lights.' Even into the 1980s, the Corvette continued to be the stuff of the rock ballads. Pop singer Prince wailed in his 1983 hit about a 'Little Red Corvette,' although he has never owned one.

In addition to being in the entertainment spotlight, the Corvette's mystique is supported by a large cadre of fanatics who adore the car. There are more than 500 Corvette fan clubs of varying size and on any

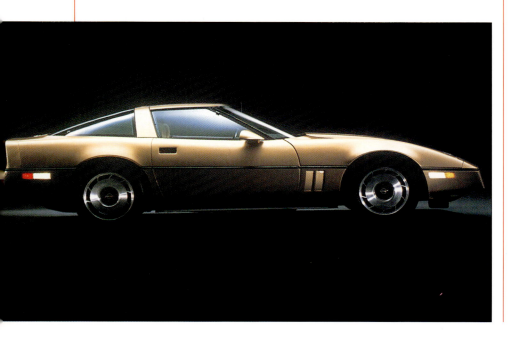

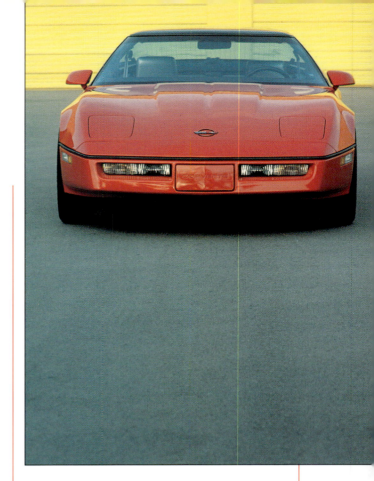

weekend in every state there's a Corvette show or some other gathering of Corvette owners.

Each year in Bloomington, Illinois, the elite Corvettes of the world gather for a concours called Bloomington Gold. The four-day concours is deep cathartic therapy for Corvette fans. One of the highlights is a driving tour in which 650 Corvettes of all years parade over a 21-mile route.

Some owners are quiet types, content to drive their cars and frequently polish the fiberglass flanks. A significant portion of owners, however, are fanatics who live and breathe Corvettes. Owning one Corvette is not enough, and having 20 is not too many.

One bizarre story involves a grocer in Maine who bought a new 1954 Corvette and almost immediately recognized it as a car

RIGHT *The aggressive, hunkered-down front end of the 1985 Corvette.*

destined for greatness. He wanted to save it so he could pass it on to his infant daughter when she grew up. Toward the end, he built a vault for the car in one of his stores and bricked the Polo White Corvette up inside so it wouldn't deteriorate. He left a small window in the vault so he could gaze at the car from time to time.

The 1954 Corvette was in that vault for 27 years and, upon the grocer's death and according to his last will and testament, it was freed from the vault and given to his daughter. The story goes that the Corvette survived the

ABOVE *1988: the Corvette marque had survived for an amazing 35 years, and had gone through six major body style changes and myriad engineering improvements.*

entombment with the only noticeable damage being that the white paint had turned yellow.

More mundane stories involving Corvette fanaticism abound. Several years a go a couple from South Carolina got married standing in a red 1957 Corvette, the minister conducting the service standing in front of the car. On top of the wedding cake was – what else – a miniature Corvette.

Not only is the Corvette itself revered, but some people have benefited just by being associated with the car. That's just what happened to Tony Klieber, a Chevrolet assembly line worker who happened to be in the right place at the right time. Klieber drove the first Corvette off the assembly line in Flint, Michigan, in 1953. A photographer captured the moment and in later years Klieber became something of a folk hero.

Corvette clubs would ask Klieber to speak about what it was like to drive the first Corvette. When he retired from Chevrolet and later became ill, some Corvette fan magazines ran updates on his condition and he received hundreds of get-well cards from Corvette owners nationwide.

Why does the Corvette inspire this sort of loyalty? Why is it still the top-dog symbol car in America after nearly four decades? One easy answer is that the Corvette is unique among American cars. It is the only true two-seat sports car built by a US manufacturer.

And it has survived the years of change without swerving too far from its original concept. Given the fickle tastes of US car buyers, it's unusual for a car to remain in production for decades, much less remain as its first designers intended.

But there are other reasons, too. No other car made in America indicates success and style quite the way the Corvette does. While Cadillac, once the US standard of success, has slipped to being considered little more than a fancy Oldsmobile, the Corvette's image has been enhanced. It is the car of choice for a significant portion of the well-to-do, post-war baby boom generation.

In 1987, a survey by Knapp Communications Corporation of US car buyers with household incomes above $50,000 found that the Corvette was considered the sexiest car. 'It beat out everybody,' said Robert Brown, a Knapp vice-president. 'And I'm talking Ferrari. I'm talking Maserati. I'm talking Porsche.'

That image as a cutting-edge automobile is only going to be further boosted by the 1990 introduction of the ZR-1, a 180-mph version that is truly a contender with the likes of Lotus, Ferrari and Porsche.

And as the new Corvettes are honed into ever-sharper driving machines, almost all older Corvettes are enjoying a renaissance of sorts.

Collectors and speculators in classic cars are driving the prices for older Corvettes into the stratosphere. Corvettes that were selling for under $10,000 in 1980 are now selling for more than $100,000.

BELOW Corvette has been in and out of racing since the 1950s. In the 1980s Corvettes were simply too good for SCCA showroom stock endurance races and had to be put in a class of their very own – the Corvette Challenge.

Mitchell Kruse, owner of Kruse International, the world's largest auction house for collector cars, says that the interest in Corvettes is directly related to the phenomenal increase in prices for Ferraris.

'As Ferrari prices have risen, they have pushed up prices for Corvettes,' says Kruse.

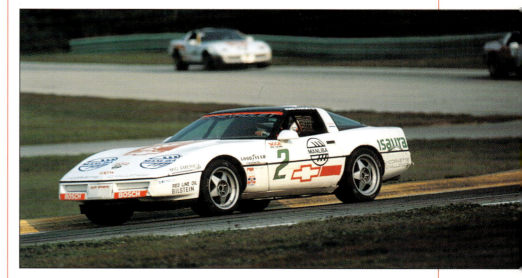

BELOW Ticking the spec boxes has often provided Corvette customers with different engine capacities, and in 1988, there was even the race-developed GTO body kit available through Chevy dealers.

And the interest is not just confined to the United States. Kruse says that Corvette buyers are coming from Japan and Europe in increasing numbers. 'The Corvette has become a worldwide car,' he says.

So a unique combination of factors – new, high-tech models, an image as a four-wheel sex symbol and a rich, lengthy history as America's only sports car – have come together to make the Corvette a world-class automobile, America's automotive heartbeat.

A DREAM CAR BECOMES REALITY

For a car that has flourished for nearly four decades, the Corvette was created on a whim and a prayer.

Consider the state of the automotive world in 1952: it was at once a simpler and more complex time. America was on top of the industrial world, its factories churning out more consumer goods than any other nation. When it came to automobiles, the US consumer had an insatiable appetite and only a car made in Detroit would do.

Longer, lower and wider was the theme of the day. Bigger was better, and there were no hints that Europe, much less Japan, would one day challenge for dominance.

If there was a fly in the ointment, it was in the quirky and ill-defined arena of 'sports cars.' Some of the millions of soldiers who had been to Europe in World War II had come back with a taste for the light, nimble open cars built in England. Two particular models had caught the fancy of a very small but highly visible number of US drivers: the MG-TD and the Jaguar XK 120.

If the Model T was the car that made the automobile accessible to the common man, the MG-TD was the common man's sports car. With its hinged cowl, tall wire wheels and tractor-like four-cylinder engine, the MG was the antithesis of the American car.

Yet thousands of people, particularly in the Northeast and in Southern California, were drawn to the attractive two-seat roadster. They revelled in its ability to scout around corners and the way it communicated a positive feel of the road. If it was a tad slow and somewhat ill-suited for the freeways

beginning to crisscross America, then that was a small trade off for the MG's other charms.

And the weak points of the MG were answered in the revolutionary Jaguar XK 120. More than twice the price of the MG, the Jaguar was clearly a step ahead of anything available in the United States. Its 3.5-liter double-overhead camshaft six-cylinder engine was in its day a technological tour de force. The Jaguar's handling was superb and it had the power that US driving conditions demanded. Sure, the brakes were less than adequate, but Detroit's cars were no better. The common man bought the MG. The wealthy and movie stars such as Clark Gable bought the Jaguar.

The man at General Motors with an eye on all these unusual cars was Harley Earl. A massive man in both stature and reputation, Earl was a General Motors vice president and head of GM's Styling Center in the early 1950s. Unlike the almost Byzantine workings of GM today, the world's largest car maker in the

1950s was dominated by a few men who wielded tremendous power.

Earl, who started with GM in 1926 under the direction of Alfred P Sloan Jr, was one of the giants at General Motors. He was first and foremost a coachbuilder and he had personal authority to leave his imprint on virtually every GM design. 'I think that Earl liked cars and pretty much had an interest in sporty cars,' says Bob Cumberford, a columnist for *Automobile* magazine who worked as a stylist at GM in the mid 1950s. 'He was not in any way a bureaucrat.'

His taste for wild and outrageous designs had its showcase in a traveling GM roadshow called Motorama. This annual display was part circus, part sales too. Alongside the latest GM production models, a few special cars always appeared. These were 'dream cars,' vehicles that were meant to tantalize the car buyers but which were unlikely to see production.

In mid 1952, sports cars were very much on Earl's mind. His college-age son, Jerry, was captivated by cars such as the Jaguar. Earl was as an astute judge of automotive trends and he believed that GM needed its own sports car. Unlike today, when proposals for new cars must clear endless hurdles, almost all it took in 1952 was Earl's hunch that America wanted a GM-two seater.

An effort at building a massive two-seater – a car called the Le Sabre that was shown at the 1951 Motorama – had met with some interest but was almost universally panned by sports car watchers as being too, too much. With that in mind, on June 2, 1952, Earl cut the orders at the GM Styling Center for Project Opel, a much more sports car-oriented vehicle that was to become the Corvette.

'The Corvette was pretty clearly Harley Earl's whim and desire. What Earl wanted, Earl got done. But somewhere along the way

he got a lot of other people interested in it,' says Cumberford.

Project Opel was to be a two-seater built on the same 102-inch wheelbase as the Jaguar XK 120. It would be the featured car of the 1953 Motorama and, with a definite eye toward possible production, Project Opel would be outfitted with Chevrolet running gear.

In addition to Earl, the other major force behind Project Opel was Edward N Cole, who

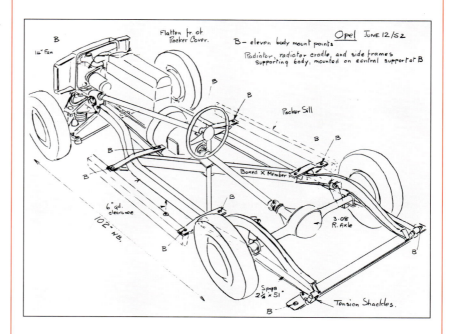

was new to Chevrolet in 1952 as that division's chief engineer. Early in Project Opel, Earl went to Cole to give a preview of the show car. Cole was a kindred spirit, having owned a Jaguar XK 120 and a Cadillac-Allard.

Cole signed on to Earl's project when he was shown the plaster Opel mockup. What Cole saw was a two-seat roadster with simple, unadorned lines. The two-seat cockpit as positioned just forward of the rear axle, and the engine would sit low and back toward the cockpit. There were no roll-up windows and there was, for 1952, a paucity of chrome.

With a mandate to use as many off-the-shelf parts as possible, Chevrolet set about animating Project Opel. At the heart of the car was an X-type frame designed exclusively for Project Opel. At the back, there were two four-leaf springs, while the independent front suspension was built around coil springs.

LEFT Head of GM Styling, 'Misterl' would be the man who made the Corvette a reality. He was closely involved with the project for many years: this is a '63 plate.

ABOVE The original sketch for the 'Opel' frame, penned by Maurice Olley in the summer of 1952; a twin-rail unit with a central X member for strength.

The front subassembly was virtually unchanged from the system introduced by Chevrolet in 1934, though it was designed to ride very low. One of the other concessions to the car's sporting nature was a stiffer front sway bar.

Chevrolet chose to use its workhorse six-cylinder engine as the powerplant. When word of this leaked out, Chevrolet was criticized for using an engine that dated back to 1937. But the straight six that was installed in the first Corvette was as modern as any American engine in its day.

The Blue-Flame Six, as it was dubbed when the Corvette debuted, had a bore and stroke of 3.562×3.937, resulting in a displacement of 3,861cc. The engine had a fully pressurized oiling system and a compression ratio of eight to one. Through the use of a special camshaft that peaked at 4,200 rpm, a more efficient exhaust manifold and three sidedraft Carter carburetors, horsepower was boosted to 150 (optimistically rated at 160 in the prototype), up from the 108 horsepower normally available from that engine.

More controversial than the use of a somewhat mundane six-cylinder engine was the exclusive use of a two-speed Powerglide automatic transmission. This question can be fairly asked: Why would Earl, Cole, GM, Chevrolet, *et al*, put an automatic transmission in a sports car when the nature of most sports cars demanded manual-shift transmissions?

There are several ways that question can be answered. In 1953, the automatic transmission was a new gadget, something that was an extra-cost option. In keeping with the theme of Motorama cars – to showcase GM technology – the Powerglide was a logical choice. But more to the point, GM undoubtedly saw the use of Powerglide as a way to broaden the sports car market, which at the time probably represented fewer than 5,000 sales worldwide.

In a June, 1954 article, *Road & Track* magazine quoted a GM engineer and former Rolls-Royce chassis designer, Maurice Olley, on the use of the Powerglide automatic in the Corvette: 'The use of an automatic

RIGHT *Nobody – not even Harley Earl – could have known in 1953 that the Corvette was here to stay; by 1957, however, GM was distributing* Corvette News *to thousands of enthusiasts.*

RIGHT *"The magic of fiber glass," trumpets* Corvette News: *the body is lowered onto the chassis of a '57 . . . "the ignition is switched on and the Corvette draws its first deep breath."*

BELOW *In 1953, Chevrolet didn't have a V-8: what they did have was the Blue Flame Six. Chevrolet's chief engineer Ed Cole managed to hop up the stock engine's 115 bhp to 150 bhp.*

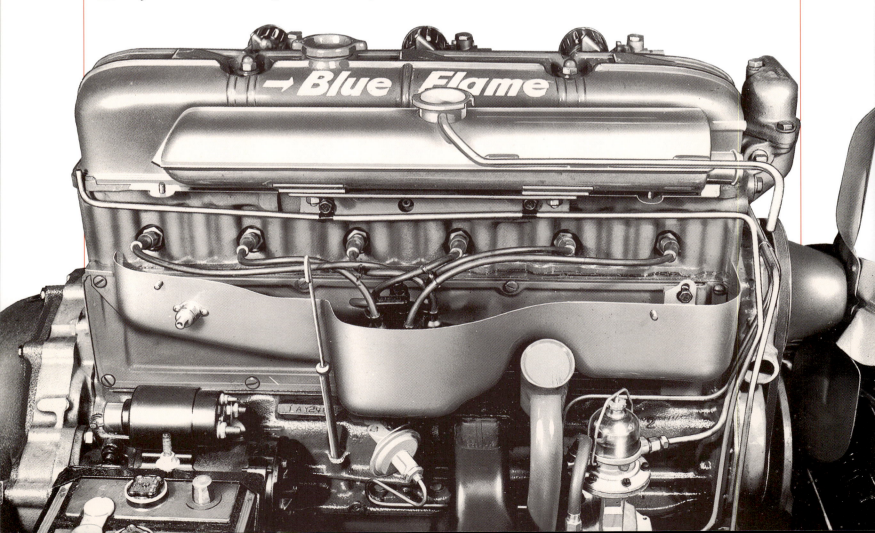

transmission has been criticized by those who believe that sports car enthusiasts want nothing but a four-speed crash shift. The answer is that the typical sports car enthusiast, like the 'average' man, or the square root of minus one, is an imaginary quantity. Also, as the sports car appeals to a wider section of the public, the center of gravity of this theoretical individual is shifting from the austerity of the pioneer towards the luxury of modern ideas . . . there is no need to apologize for the performance of this car with its automatic transmission.

The rest of the Opel/Corvette running gear was unremarkable. A Hotchkiss driveline was used (as opposed to the then more traditional torque tube), and the live rear axle carried

3.27 to 1 gearing. Steering was a Saginaw box with a slightly tweaked 16 to 1 ratio. The brakes were standard Chevrolet 11-inch drums, although the master cylinder system was beefed-up.

With the chassis and drivetrain set, the other aspect of the Corvette that was to make it remarkable emerged: the fiberglass body.

Fiberglass – or Glass Reinforced Plastic, as it was also called – had been used by GM Styling for mock-ups and show cars before Project Opel. So the fact that the Motorama Corvette prototype was made of fiberglass was not surprising. What made fiberglass the body material of choice was GM's desire to put the Corvette into production as quickly as possible. It would have taken too long to gear up for the Kirksite dies necessary to stamp out steel bodies.

Initially, only the limited production run of 300 Corvettes in 1953 was to have been of fiberglass. Starting with the '54 model, steel bodies were to have become the norm. But the public came to think of fiberglass as a high-tech material and this fitted well with the Corvette's image. Perhaps more importantly, a process using matched metal dies to mold and quickly cure the fiberglass was developed that gave consistent, quality fiberglass body parts. Steel Corvettes have never appeared.

When Project Opel, renamed Corvette after a fast type of warship, debuted January 17 in New York at the Motorama, Earl's gut

ABOVE AND LEFT
Automatic transmission, red trim and polo white bodywork were the only options in 1953; the tiny pilot assembly plant in Flint, Michigan, simply couldn't handle the ticking of any specification boxes by individual buyers.

CORVETTE SHOWDOWN		
	1953 CORVETTE	**1953 MG TD**
Price	$3,498	$2,157
Dimensions		
Wheelbase (inches)	102	94
Length (inches)	167	140
Weight (pounds)	2,705	2,005
Engine and Drivetrain type	In-line six	In-line four
Displacement (c.i.)	235.5	76.3
Horsepower	150	54
Transmission	Two-speed automatic	Four-speed manual
Performance		
0–60 mph	11 seconds	19.4 seconds
Top Speed	106 mph	80 mph

BELOW AND RIGHT On all Corvettes from 1953 to 1955, the headlamps were recessed behind mesh screens, and the body sides were flat.

Chevrolet began production of the first Corvettes on a tiny assembly line in Flint, Michigan, in June of 1953. Only three Corvettes a day could be produced at the plant, which was a stopgap facility until production could be moved to St Louis, Missouri. Due to the makeshift nature of the Flint facility, all of the 300 cars built in 1953

instincts were confirmed: America loved the idea of the Corvette.

Thousands of people, spurred on by heavy-handed hints that the Corvette was headed into production, signed up to buy. Fears that the automatic transmission and six-cylinder engine would detract from its appeal were at first groundless. Potential buyers fell in love with the low, sexy look of the Corvette. Compared to the tall, boxy cars in Chevrolet's line-up, the Corvette was straight out of a Buck Rogers space fantasy. Any disappointments in the car would not come until they were on the road.

were identical – white with red interiors. Workers literally glued the cars' bodies together and individually sanded and painted them. At a price of $3,498, the first Corvettes were the most expensive Chevrolets ever. However, in line with the implied target of competing with the likes of Jaguar, the

LEFT AND ABOVE LEFT *The bodies were only actually built up, finished at Flint: the preparation of the fiberglass – the die pressing and trimming – was done at Morrison's Molded Fiber Glass Body Company, in Ashtabula, Ohio.*

TOP AND ABOVE *The Flint assembly plant occupied a single floor of the old customer delivery garage; it was a temporary operation designed to iron out the bugs before production began in earnest in St. Louis. The line could produce three cars a day.*

Corvette was still more than $500 cheaper than the XK 120 in America.

Demand for those first few Corvettes was so huge that Chevrolet in effect parceled them out to the 'right people.' Recognizing that image was a crucial component to the Corvette, Chervolet pushed its dealers to sell the first cars to local celebrities and community leaders: buyers whose only recommendation was that they had the necessary cash would have to wait for 1954 models.

That plan appeared to backfire on Chevrolet, as the Corvette's natural flaws began to emerge just as full-scale production of the '54 models began rolling. Since the first cars were in the hands of people in the news spotlight, their complaints received more widespread distribution. By the time the Corvette was available to the average man, its image had been tarnished.

Complaints about the Corvette were both objective and subjective. Features that were overlooked in a show car became unacceptable in a real-world vehicle. Most owners hadn't considered the problems associated with a true roadster, particularly during cold-weather months. The top was unwieldy and, even with the side curtains in place, rain poured in when the car travelled at speed. There were no outside door handles and there were no door locks. Power was merely adequate, although the handling was within the bounds of a sports car. American buyers wanted their cars with all the comforts, and many felt the first Corvettes had too many inconveniences. In fairness, the people who felt this way probably had little past contact with sports cars.

But those sports car enthusiasts who were willing to put up with a damp interior in exchange for some speed and decent handling weren't in love with the Corvette, either. They just couldn't forgive Chevrolet for offering a sports car with only an automatic transmission and they were suspicious of a sports car with such a down-home pedigree. Earl's dream car became the butt of an awful lot of jokes.

In those unliberated days, the Corvette was frequently referred to as 'a ladies car,' for any real man would demand a manual gearshift in his sports car. It's ironic that by 1990, when the Corvette can legitimately challenge any sports car in the world, 80 per cent of production is automatic-equipped cars.

With the negative reactions starting to show, demand for the Corvette slipped dramatically. When full production was shifted to a Chevrolet plant in St Louis, the sales lull set in. By the end of the 1954 sales year, more than 3,600 Corvettes had been produced. The only problem was that dealers still had more than 1,000 of them on their lots and were begging for sales. Even the cut in price made possible by the economies of larger production – from $3,498 in 1953 to $2,774 in 1954 – was not enough to goose sales at all.

With such a large percentage of '54 Corvettes unsold, the money-minded people at Chevrolet moved to cut their losses and the Corvette's future looked dim. Plans for a

ABOVE *With the negative publicity surrounding the '54 Corvette, GM had plenty of spare cars for such publicity shots. By the end of 1954, 1,076 cars were sitting in the lots unsold, from a total production of 3,600.*

LEFT *In addition to the roadster, several Corvette variations were built, such as the fastback Corvair, a 1954 Motorama show car.*

RIGHT *The Corvair may well have made it into production if the Corvette roadster sales had not been so frightening to GM's accountants in 1954.*

BELOW RIGHT *No restyle for 1955 – but under the skin, the now legendary small-block V-8. 0–60 times were two seconds faster than with the Blue Flame Six, at 8.5–9.0 seconds.*

BELOW LEFT *In the foreground, the Corvair; mid-ground, the 1954/55 Nomad, which would reappear as a full-size Chevy; and in the distance the standard roadster (right) and a proposed removable hardtop version (left).*

redesigned model in '55 were shelved and none was produced until the unsold '54 models were gone. So in 1955, total sales were a dismal 700 cars.

Before ringing in the changes that saved the Corvette, it is instructive to look back at how the Corvette truly compared to its competitors. As seen from a nearly 40-year perspective, the first Corvette seems like a car that was just misunderstood. Consider the comparison with the Jaguar XK 120, clearly the car that Earl and Cole had in mind as the Corvette's nearest competitor. As had been pointed out, the Corvette and Jaguar shared the same wheelbase of 102 inches. But the similarities went beyond that.

The Jaguar used a 3442cc six-cylinder engine, compared to the slightly larger 3861cc six in the Corvette. Using sophisticated double overhead camshafts, Jaguar pumped 160 horsepower from its engine. The larger but more conventional Corvette engine produced 150 horsepower.

Both cars used large-diameter drum brakes and were traditional two-seat roadsters with plastic side curtains. Where the Jaguar had the edge was in the elegant design and appointments in its interior. The Corvette looked mass-produced, with its metal dash and poorly placed gauges.

Further, the Jaguar had all the right sports car extras – wire wheels as opposed to the fake spinner hubcaps on the Corvette, optional rear gear ratios and, of course, the *de rigeur* four-speed manual gearbox. Added to that was a plethora of extras, from larger gas tanks to close-ratio gearboxes, to make the Jaguar competitive as a weekend racer.

Chevrolet would eventually learn the value of competition as a way to sell the Corvette, but in the early 1950s GM still clung to the corporate mandate of no racing. However, several private entries did show up at amateur events and they proved the Corvette had some basic talents.

In its July, 1955 edition, *Road & Track* had this observation: 'Watching a Corvette in an airport race coming into a corner with fast company, we have observed that the brakes show up poorly, but the actual cornering is done just as fast, flat and comfortably as several imported sports cars we could name.'

Still, the base Corvette and the base XK 120 were close in terms of bottom-line performance. The Corvette reached 60 mph in 11 seconds and had a top speed of 107 mph.

C O R V E T T E S H O W D O W N		
	1954 CORVETTE	**JAGUAR XK 120**
Price	$2,774	$3,700
Dimensions		
Wheelbase (inches)	102	102
Length (inches)	167	174
Weight (pounds)	2,705	2,855
Engine and Drivetrain type	In-line six	DOHC six
Displacement (c.i.)	235.5	210
Horsepower	150	160
Transmission	Two-speed automatic	Four-speed manual
Performance		
0–60 mph	11 seconds	10 seconds
Top Speed	106 mph	120 mph

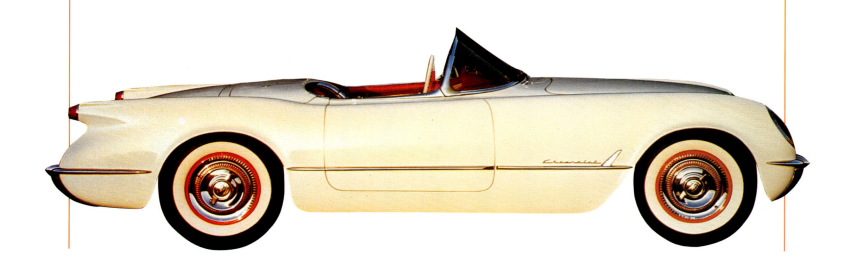

The Jaguar was a second quicker to 60 mph and had a top speed of 120 mph.

The '54–'55 Corvette was clearly a bargain, selling for $1,200 less than the XK 120. Yet that difference in price was not enough to persuade potential buyers to choose the Chevrolet over the Jaguar. Sports cars were luxuries, and if someone was going to spend $3,000 on one, another $1,200 was a small price to pay for a car that carried more cachet.

inches – 4,344cc – and, in the Corvette, produced 195 horsepower through the use of a tuned camshaft and a four-barrel carburetor. Although technically an option, virtually all of the '55 Corvettes came with the Turbo-Fire V-8.

The other change for 1955 – at last – was the availability of a manual transmission. However, the three-speed gearbox was offered so late in the year that only about two dozen cars received it.

BELOW Nine '54 Corvettes parading at the race track; the poor sales figures for 1955, despite the introduction of V-8 power – a mere 700 units – are of course partly explained by the need to shift all those '54s through the salesrooms.

Faced with snail-like sales of the Corvette by the start of the 1955 sales year, Cole and others at Chevrolet knew their car needed a boost. The most noticeable help came in the birth of the small-block Chevrolet V-8. When the Corvette was first put together, the in-line six was the only production engine Cole had available. In the race toward V-8 power, Chevrolet was noticeably behind its contemporaries, particularly Ford.

But when the Chevy V-8 debuted in 1955, it was a sweet powerplant that was well worth the wait. Its displacement was 265 cubic

Addition of the V-8 turned the Corvette into a true high-performance automobile. Zero to 60 mph times dropped sharply, from 11 seconds on the six-cylinder cars to 8.7 seconds with the V-8. Top speed jumped to 119 mph.

The brakes were still weak and there were no answers to the complaints about rain leaks, no door handles or locks and general gripes about workmanship. But with the V-8, the Corvette was a speed contender and it gained considerable respect in the eyes of many sports car enthusiasts.

RIGHT Saved by the competition; it was the introduction of the Thunderbird by the arch enemy, Ford, in 1955, that was instrumental in salvaging the Corvette dream. Chevrolet simply couldn't leave Ford all alone in the sports car market.

Despite the big image boost, the Corvette was on thin ice until Chevrolet's chief rival, Ford, upped the ante with the 1955 Thunderbird. The Thunderbird was strong in all the places the Corvette was weak. The T-Bird with a two-seater that had roll-up windows, conventional door handles and

ABOVE *For 1954, it was no longer the case that you could have a Corvette in any color so long as it was white; blue, red and black were available options.*

locks, an optional hardtop, V-8 power and the choice of a three-speed automatic or a three-speed manual.

Longer and heavier than the Corvette, the Thunderbird was not a true sports car. 'The Thunderbird was a convertible, it wasn't a sports car,' says Robert Cumberford. 'The Thunderbird could never be driven on a race track against a Corvette because its chassis was so soggy.'

Perhaps because it was meant for boulevards, not race tracks, the Thunderbird appealed to that cadre of buyers Harley Earl suspected was out there. Ford sold 16,000 Thunderbirds in 1955, more than four times the Corvettes built to that date. And although Chevrolet had a myopic view of the value of competition on the race track, there was no race they were more determined to win than a sales race with Ford. It just wouldn't do to fold the Corvette's tent in the face of competition from Ford. The Corvette would just have to get better and stake out its ground.

ZORA TO THE RESCUE

3

As much as Harley Earl gets credit for creating the Corvette, the man whose name is still most closely aligned with the car is that of Zora Arkus-Duntov.

An opinionated genius of an automotive engineer, Duntov joined the Corvette team in 1953. As the Corvette teetered on the brink of bankruptcy, Duntov and Edward N Cole collaborated on how to save the car. Born in Belgium, Duntov had raced Porsches at Le Mans, and naturally brought a strong European outlook to the Corvette. While he had minor influences on the original Corvettes, his stamp was firmly planted on the '56 Corvette. He knew that what the Corvette needed was a healthy dose of horsepower and handling.

In terms of styling and creature comforts, the '56 Corvette was the first serious attempt to answer the criticisms that had nearly killed the '53–'55 cars. Clare MacKichan, who was head of the Chevrolet styling studio, and Bob Cadaret worked on the problems. Roll-up

ABOVE *Zora Arkus-Duntov behind the wheel of the SS racer; the Belgian-born engineer had been on the Corvette program from 1953, but from 1956 he would become the central figure in the turnaround of the Corvette's fortunes.*

windows – either manually operated or with optional power lifts – door handles and a fresh-air heater appeared. The convertible top was redesigned, and it too was available with a power lift.

The wheelbase remained at 102 inches, but most everything else about the body changed. The rear end was more rounded, and the tail lights became integrated into the

design. Up front, the single headlights were set into forward-thrusting fairings and there were power bulges in the hood. A hardtop was offered to increase the car's cold-weather appeal.

A design cue that was to become the car's trademark into the early 1960s was the use of scooped-out coves running from the front wheel wells back to the middle of the doors. The coves, when painted in a contrasting color, were arguably the most stylish touch on the new Corvette, giving it a very aggressive appearance.

The styling aside, it was Duntov's work on the basics of the Corvette that made the '56 model something more than a reskinned Motorama project vehicle. Some fine-tuning of the suspension improved the handling, but the biggest improvements were in the arena of raw power.

The promised three-speed manual transmission finally appeared as an option to

ABOVE The scooped-out sides of the 1956 design were such an integral part of the body that they could be highlighted with a chrome strip and contrasting color, without looking self-conscious.

LEFT The SR-2 show car was created in the same year, and made its racing debut at Sebring in 1957.

the Powerglide, and the misunderstood Blue Flame Six became history, replaced by two new versions of the 265-cubic-inch V-8. One version used a single four-barrel carburetor to pump out 195 horsepower, and the other used dual four-barrels to create an awesome 225 horsepower.

With the high-output engine, the Corvette became the meanest, fastest machine in the land. Road tests of the time pegged the zero-to-60 mph sprint at a tick more than seven seconds, with a top speed of 129 mph. With all this new power and the manual gearbox, the Corvette could at last be considered a contender on the race track. Duntov, an advocate of the link between racing success and high sales, set out to prove that his improved Corvette was a winner.

When it came to speed, Daytona Beach, Florida, was the place to flex your muscles. Each year the hard-packed sand beach was marked off and cars of all manner made straight, top-speed runs. The location had become famous for stock car races, which were initially held on the beach and then moved to the spectacular high-banked speed way in 1959.

Early in 1956, Duntov, with the enthusiastic support of Cole – who by 1956 had assumed the reins at Chevrolet – traveled to Daytona for a crack at the top-speed crown. Building on a '54 Corvette that was a prototype for the '55 V-8 car, Duntov began to try to cheat the wind. He installed a wing-like headrest similar to the D-Type Jaguar, a Brooklands windscreen and rounded headlight covers. Once the drag was sufficiently reduced, he installed a heavily modified V-8 that relied on a Duntov-designed camshaft to produce 255 horsepower.

At the beach, Duntov flew by at 150 mph, becoming the fastest passenger car there that year. More production-oriented Corvettes driven by John Fitch and Betty Skelton also showed well.

On the heels of that accomplishment, a team of Corvettes with lukewarm factory sponsorship tackled the famed endurance race at Sebring, Florida. Although still no match for the elite sports cars of the world – Aston Martin, Ferrari, Maserati or Jaguar – one Corvette managed to finish 15th and capture its class.

Speed, new styling and the added oomph from some honest racing efforts breathed new life into the Corvette. Compared to the dismal 700 cars sold in 1955, the '56 Corvette was a

C O R V E T T E S H O W D O W N		
	1956 CORVETTE	**1956 THUNDERBIRD**
Price	$3,149	$2,695
Dimensions		
Wheelbase (inches)	102	102
Length (inches)	168	175.3
Weight (pounds)	2,850	3,240
Engine and Drivetrain type	Pushrod V-8	Pushrod V-8
Displacement (c.i.)	265	292
Horsepower	210	198
Transmission	Three-speed manual	Three-speed automatic
Performance		
0–60 mph	7.5 seconds	9.5 seconds
Top Speed	119 mph	112 mph

world-beater. Chevrolet managed to sell 3467 of them that year. Still, the car's future was not assured. 'A redesign originally slated for the '57 model was put off,' says Cumberford, who worked on the project. 'The reason that the '56 design ran two years was that the body engineers had to do a new hood for the pickup truck and that was more important than the whole Corvette,' he adds.

In fact, concern about the fate of the Corvette was so high that Cumberford and others took the initiative to try to broaden the car's appeal. 'In 1956 there was talk of killing off the Corvette and that's when Tony Lapine, Stan Mott and I did a big concerted effort to make a four-passenger Corvette, because we knew we could sell more of those,' Cumberford says. 'It would have been a 108-inch wheelbase car with a long hood and a short rear deck. We used Tony Lapine's home address for an unofficial survey we mailed out to a bunch of sports car people all over the country. We asked them what they thought of a four-passenger sports car. We got all this positive stuff back and took it to Harley Earl, who told us we were paid to design, not think.'

As a postscript, Cumberford says that he, Lapine and Mott had even named the new four-place Corvette: the Mustang.

ABOVE. *The Ramjet FI smallblock was one of the best engines in America from 1957 to 1965, when production ceased.*

Fortunately, the people who wanted to kill off the Corvette were unsuccessful and for 1957 Corvette continued its theme of more power. What was to become a landmark engine was introduced: the 283-cubic-inch

RIGHT *"283/283": 1957 was the year of the fuelie – the fuel-injected V-8 that produced one horsepower per cubic inch.*

OPPOSITE *Sports car looks, and at last undeniable sports car performance for 1956.*

fuel-injected V-8. Using a mechanical injection system – as opposed to the computer-managed systems of today – the 283 managed the considerable feat of producing one horsepower for every cubic inch, and some people claimed output was actually a few ponies higher.

Developed by Duntov and others at the urging of Cole, the fuel-injection system used mechanically triggered air and fuel meters to deliver vaporized gasoline to each cylinder. As revolutionary as the use of fiberglass had been in the first Corvette, the introduction of fuel injection was also seen as a cutting-edge development. As *Road & Track* wrote in its August, 1957, edition: 'The fuel-injection engine is an absolute jewel, quiet and remarkably docile when driven around town,

yet instantly transformable into a roaring brute when pushed hard.'

Combined with the four-speed transmission that also became available in '57, the Positraction limited-slip differential and revised suspension handling packages, Corvette finally vanquished any doubts that it was a formidable package.

In its most muscular form, the Corvette could hit 60 mph in 5.7 seconds and run the quarter mile in 14.3 seconds. Those figures are all the more remarkable because they are nearly identical to the performance figures of the 1989 L98 Corvette. Admittedly the newer Corvette is by far the better-mannered vehicle, but the '57 Fuelie was a rocketship.

Although only about 1000 of the Corvettes sold in 1957 had the fuel-injection engine under the hood, the glamour of the powerhouse engine undoubtedly contributed

BELOW *How to spot a 1957 Corvette: a full set of 13 "teeth" in the grille – for 1958, there were just nine.*

ABOVE *The 1958 Corvette was longer, heavier and wider than its predecessor. New colors were offered; charcoal, silver-blue, turquoise, and yellow.*

to sharp increase in sales of 6,339 cars, nearly double the 1956 sales and nearly 10 times the number of Corvettes sold in 1955.

That the Corvette was becoming a hit was evident. What was perhaps not so evident was where all these new Corvette buyers were coming from. Harley Earl's hunch that the Corvette would broaden the sports car market was on target, but a few years premature.

Corvette buyers were for the most part not deep-dyed sports car enthusiasts who eagerly traded their Jaguars or Maseratis. Fans of European sports cars still had a snobbish view of the Corvette. It was sold alongside Bel Air sedans, they reasoned, so it couldn't be a true sports car.

What helped boost the success of the Corvette was the growing middle and upper-middle class in America. More and more people had what would come to be called 'discretionary income'. Success was often measured by the car you drove and the Corvette played to that image. But to dismiss the Corvette as a glitzy toy would be grossly unfair. Compared to some of the well-regarded sports cars of its day, the Corvette was a champion.

It was faster than all but the most exotic Ferraris and Aston Martins, easily outdistancing the then-new Austin-Healey, the MGA and the Triumph TR3, Though not as nimble, and much heavier than most European sports cars, the Corvette was well-balanced and its handling was flat and predictable.

And at a price of about $4,000 for a loaded fuel-injection model, it was a relative bargain. The Jaguar XK 150, which was slower than the Corvette, sold for about $5,000 in the United States, with an Aston-Martin fetching more than $6,000. A Mercedes 190 SL sold for about the same price as the Corvette, but offered only mediocre performance. With a growing cadre of supporters, the Corvette was in the ballgame to stay, and sales grew sharply.

The 1958 model, which was distinguished on the outside by the introduction of quad headlights and the tacky addition of chrome runners on the trunk lid and fake louvers on the hood, continued the success. More than 9,100 people took home Corvettes that year.

What they got for their money was a still further improved car, though heavier and wider. Acting on complaints from Duntov, the

interior of the '58 model was brought up to the potential of the rest of the car. All of the instruments were grouped in front of the driver and the steering column was shortened. A center console was also added.

Continuing the Detroit theme of more power, the 283 fuel-injection engine had a top power rating of 290 horsepower, with a 250-horsepower version available, as well as the 230-horsepower base carbureted version.

When the 1959 model appeared, the chrome fad was on the way out and the metal strips added to the '58 Corvette were relegated to the scrap heap. Notable changes included the introduction of a reverse-gear lockout on the manual-transmission cars and a new rear suspension that used radius arms to lessen rear axle hop under acceleration.

As a concession to the growing number of amateur Corvette racers, an upgraded brake package, RPO 686, was offered. Using linings that were sintered-metallic and polished drums, the new system was suitable for street use yet held up better under the high temperatures and stress of racing.

When the Corvette entered the '60s, it had come a long way from the Powerglide car of '53. It was a blindingly fast car that was a respected competitor on the race track. Its future was assured by the slow upward spiral of its sales.

Though there was talk of a new Corvette that would be as radical as the first one had been, it was still a few years off when the '60 Corvette debuted. The '60 Corvette was a car of refinements, not revolution.

The engine offerings remained essentially unchanged after Chevrolet cancelled plans to offer an aluminium cylinder head package that boosted the 283-cubic-inch horsepower to 315. The spirit of Chevrolet was willing, but the production line technology couldn't cope with the finesse it took to reliably build such an engine.

Corvette advertised 315 bhp for the top-line powerplant with aluminum heads; but the heads were cancelled and horsepower did not improve on 1959 figures – 250 and 290.

C O R V E T T E S H O W D O W N		
	1959 CORVETTE	**1959 MERCEDES 190SL**
Price	$3,700	$4,000
Dimensions		
Wheelbase (inches)	102	94.5
Length (inches)	178	169
Weight (pounds)	3,370	2,515
Engine and Drivetrain type	Fuel-injected V-8	In-line four
Displacement (c.i.)	283	116
Horsepower	290	120
Transmission	Four-speed manual	Four-speed manual
Performance		
0–60 mph	6.6 seconds	13 seconds
Top Speed	128 mph	102 mph

Undoubtedly the biggest improvement in the '60 model was the taming of its harsh-riding suspension. Duntov sought to find a happy middle ground between the flat cornering necessary for racing and the desire for a car that wouldn't dislodge the fillings in your teeth during a trip to the supermarket.

BELOW 1961 was Bill Mitchell's baby, with light, flowing lines, ducktail, and toning down of chrome.

CORVETTE SHOWDOWN		
	1961 CORVETTE	**1961 HEALEY 3000**
Price	$3,934	$3,565
Dimensions		
Wheelbase (inches)	102	92
Length (inches)	177.7	157.5
Weight (pounds)	3,080	2,460
Engine and Drivetrain type	Fuel-injected V-8	In-line six
Displacement (c.i.)	283	178
Horsepower	315	132
Transmission	Four-speed manual	Four-speed manual
Performance		
0–60 mph	6.6 seconds	9.8 seconds
Top Speed	128 mph	113 mph

Through a combination of softer springs and the use of hefty anti-roll bars at the front and rear of the car, he was able to create a Corvette that was more user-friendly than any of its predecessors. People responded and the Corvette – with a base price of $3,872 – topped the 10,000 sales mark for the first time.

The introduction of the 1961 Corvette was a landmark, although few buyers were aware of it at the time. Harley Earl, the man whose marketing and design sense had created the Corvette, had retired from General Motors in 1959. He had passed the baton at the Styling Center to William L Mitchell.

Even as the hand-picked successor, Mitchell was a very different man from Earl.

Earl was a visionary who relied heavily on others to transform his broad-bushed ideas into reality. Mitchell was no less of a visionary than Earl, but was also an accomplished artist and stylist.

The 1960 Corvette marked the first inroads that Mitchell made on the Corvette styling and as a hint of the stunning StingRay that would debut in 1963. Chrome continued its decline on American cars and the '61 Corvette was no exception. The chrome headlight bezels were gone, as was the toothy grill. But most notable was the ducktail styling on the Corvette.

Derived from the XP-700 show car and the StingRay race car prototype, the rear of the '61 Corvette was a flat deck with sharp creases above the wheel wells and small fender sweeps. It was a strange mix of a very modern rear design with a front end that was born in the mid-1950s.

To go with this new direction in design, the 315-horsepower fuel-injection engine

RIGHT Mitchell's XP-700 show car had featured the same ducktail as on the 1961 model.

OPPOSITE Even more restraint for 1962: the contrasting color option has gone. This was the last year for the open headlight.

ABOVE AND LEFT

It is obvious just how radical the new design was for 1963 when it's shown side by side with a '62. The results of extensive testing at the Cal Tech wind tunnel are manifest.

appeared, thanks to cast-iron cylinder heads based on the delicate all-aluminium design of the year before. Performance naturally improved, and the 315-horsepower Corvette could get to 60 mph in just 5.5 seconds.

The 1962 Corvette received a mild makeover from Mitchell, who was concentrating on the 1963 Sting Ray. Gone was the two-tone paint scheme for the side coves. The chrome bezels on the fake side inlets were vanquished in favor of more realistic-looking ducts (still fake).

In the quest for more horsepower, the 283-cubic-inch engine was retired in favor of a new version based on the same block. Displacing 327-cubic-inches, the new engine had a bigger bore and a longer stroke and was more comfortable with the demands made of it.

The compression ratio ranged from 10.5–to–1 to 11.25–to–1. The two-four-barrel option was dropped in favor of a smoother but no less potent single Carter four-barrel. Using big-valve cylinder heads and the top compression ratio, the fuel-injection version of the 327 pumped out 360 horsepower. The 1962 was to be the last of the cars based on the solid-axle design created by Harley Earl. Nine years earlier it had been a slightly anaemic six-cylinder car that in many respects was a rebodied family car.

By the end of its reign, the solid-axle Corvette had finally earned recognition as a quality sports car. In its test of a '61 Corvette, *Road & Track* had this to say about the Corvette: 'Continual refinements since 1954 have made the Corvette into a sports car for which no owner need make excuses.'

Corvette News (vol. V, no. 5) of 1962 included a feature on Route 66, *the popular TV show starring Martin Milner and George Maharis. Top billing went to a Corvette. Co-creator of the show Stirling Silliphant explains that "the stories are about the people who made this country great, and about two young men who are searching for identity and meaning." (It's probably better to explore the larger metaphysical questions in a Corvette than a pickup truck.)*

CORVETTE GOES RACING... SORT OF

Where the Corvette was concerned, General Motors was nearly schizophrenic on the subject of racing. Unlike Europe, where auto racing is a natural extension of automotive development and a powerful sales tool, US car makers have tended to think of racing as a minor activity.

With some notable exceptions – the assault on Le Mans by Ford in the 1960s, for one – manufacturers have kept racing at a distance from the front office. Stock car racing is perhaps the venue most supported by the factories, and even there the link is mostly through independent teams. But even given the arms-length attitude of Ford or Chrysler in the '50s, the posture at Chevrolet was downright prudish.

When the Corvette went on sale in 1953, there were no plans to take the car racing under the official Chevrolet banner. There certainly were hopes that some privateers would enter the Corvette in a few amateur races and that the cars would do well.

BELOW John Fitch, in a specially modified 1956 Corvette at Daytona Beach, Florida. The car won the modified class at the Speed Weeks trials with a two-pass average of 145.543 mph. The GM ad men loved it: "Bring on the hay bales!" shouted the copy in the magazines.

But as far as any major assault on the race track, the feeling in the corporate offices was that GM didn't need the boost that a winning race program might provide. Probably more to the point, GM didn't want the black eye that could come from a botched effort on the track.

So the Corvette in its first few years was left to soldier on and try to gain a serious reputation as a sports car without race experience.

Zora Arkus-Duntov knew that GM's ostrich-like position on racing would just not do if the Corvette was to succeed. The Corvette would have to bloody a few European noses in competition. Aided by Harley Earl and Edward Cole, Duntov pushed the idea of racing Corvettes. Though sceptical, the other GM executives didn't stop the Duntov effort.

The first effort by Duntov to show the world that the Corvette was more than a pretty plastic face came early in 1956, when Duntov prepared a special V-8 to capture top-

speed honors at the Daytona Beach speed trials. The Duntov Corvette flew through the measured mile at 150 mph.

Also working with Duntov was Connecticut racer John Fitch and Betty Skelton, who was also an accomplished pilot, having won the women's national aerobatics championship. Fitch took top production honors at Daytona and Skelton finished second. Buoyed by the Daytona success, Chevrolet decided that Sebring should be its next target. Duntov, aware that there was a big difference between straight-line speed runs at Daytona and the international

competition at Sebring, was not in favor of the Sebring outing.

He reasoned that what Chevy needed for Sebring was a purpose-built racing Corvette, which just didn't exist. To send a few street-based Corvettes into battle at Sebring was asking for disaster. So vocal was Duntov that responsibility for the '56 Sebring effort then fell to Fitch, who had to work with cars that were seriously overweight.

The outright disaster predicted by Duntov did not occur, but the best the ill-prepared Corvettes could manage was 15th-place.

That, however, was good enough to capture production class honors, and the Chevrolet public relations mill went to work, trumpeting the accomplishment. The American car buyer, largely unschooled in the fine points of international competition, bought the notion that the Corvette was a winner, on a par with Ferrari, Jaguar, Maserati and Mercedes.

Although racing was still a low-profile activity at Chevrolet, it was not quite the dirty word it had been before Daytona and Sebring. Shortly after Sebring, Harley Earl sent down word that he wanted another racing Corvette built. This one was a special order indeed because it was for Earl's son, Jerry, whose

interest in sports cars had helped spawn the Corvette.

It seems the younger Earl had a yen for sports car racing and had his eye on a Ferrari. Well Earl was adamant: no son of his was going to go racing in an Italian machine. The result a model called the SR-2. Eventually three SR-2 Corvettes were built – two of them all-out race cars and the third a street machine – and they exist today as testaments to an era when a top GM executive could wield immense power.

Bob Cumberford, now a columnist with *Automobile* magazine, was a junior stylist at General Motors when Earl ordered a Corvette built for his son. 'It was unseemly for a GM guy's son to be seen in a Ferrari,' says Cumberford, who worked on the SR-2 project and also helped design the car Duntov took to Daytona.

The design of Earl's SR-2 was at first based on a custom Corvette built for a Swedish prince, Cumberford says. That car had a small

The SR-2 was actually first put together as a tire scorcher for Harley Earl's son, Jerry, but its effectiveness as showcar and all-round publicity chaser was undeniable. The fin behind the driver's head was reminiscent of the Jaguar D-Type: such associations could only do the Corvette a lot of good.

The SS was a beautiful machine, but its first outing at Sebring in 1956 was a disaster: the brakes were unpredictable and the Magnesium body and exposed pipes (opposite, top) conducted heat right into the cockpit. The AMA racing ban of 1957 meant that the SS would never make it to its ultimate test at Le Mans.

shark-like fin rising up from the center of the trunk lid. The design is also derivative of the D-Type Jaguar, which had previously caught Harley Earl's attention.

Although Cumberford recalls that SR-2 was basically a stock car with a longer, custom snout, the car's current owner, Rich Mason of Carson City, Nevada, says his research leads him to believe that the custom body was fitted to the chassis from one of the 1956 Sebring race cars.

'I think that Jerry Earl first bought a stock 1956 Corvette with the idea that they were going to modify that,' comments Mason. 'But I think they already had a '56 Sebring chassis available because the car was changed and built in about a three-and-a-half week period. I just don't think they could have done all that they did in that length of time and come up with as nice a finished car as they did.'

The car first appeared in conjunction at Elkhart Lane, Wisconsin, in June, 1956. Jerry

Earl first drove the car with disappointing results, Cumberford says, and then famed Corvette racer Dick 'The Flying Dentist' Thompson drove it in the main event. Thompson's assessment of the car was that it was simply too heavy for racing. It was shipped back to the GM studio for more work.

'It was given to me to take some weight out of it,' Cumberford explains. 'I took out the windows, radio, heater, seats – all the superfluous stuff.' The stock seats were jettisoned in favor of a pair of Porsche Speedster bucket seats belonging to Cumberford.

It was during this refurbishment that the fin was removed from the middle of the trunk and Earl's car was fitted with an off-center high tail from the Corvette used at the Daytona speed trials. The high tail incorporates a headrest and conceals an integral roll bar and access to a 46-gallon fuel tank.

The SR-2 came with the suspension used on the Corvettes at Sebring, as well as special ducts to get air to the brakes and carburetion system. Special aerodynamic aids, such as nose cone covers over the front headlights, were also part of the package.

Power was from a 333-cubic-inch V-8 that at first was equipped with two four-barrels and soon after changed over to fuel injection. The V-8 was based on the small-block Corvette engine, which was then bored and stroked for more displacement.

Jerry Earl raced his SR-2 through 1957 – including an appearance at Sebring – after which it was sold to Jim Jeffords, who was racing on behalf of Nickey Chevrolet in Chicago. The car was repainted from silver

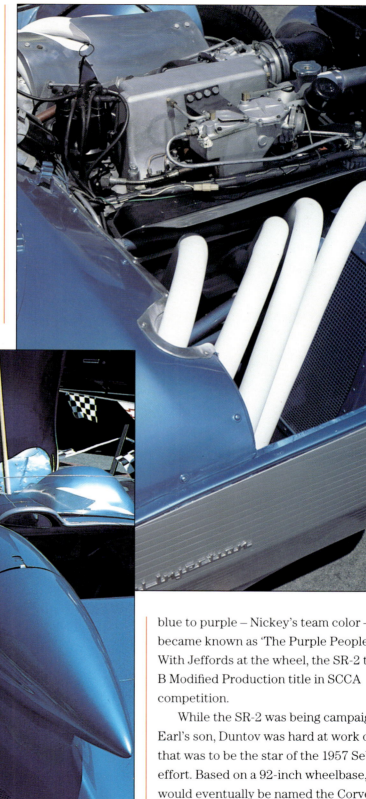

blue to purple – Nickey's team color – and became known as 'The Purple People Eater.' With Jeffords at the wheel, the SR-2 took the B Modified Production title in SCCA competition.

While the SR-2 was being campaigned by Earl's son, Duntov was hard at work on the car that was to be the star of the 1957 Sebring effort. Based on a 92-inch wheelbase, the car would eventually be named the Corvette SS.

As with most special race cars even today, the SS had very little in common with the Corvettes coming off the assembly line in St Louis. The SS started with a tubular space frame and a De Dion rear axle and an independent rear suspension. The brakes

would be drums all the way around fitted with metallic linings. New to the SS would be a complex servo system to prevent rear brake lock up, similar in theory to the computer-controlled anti-lock brake systems of today. The body was built from a super lightweight magnesium alloy and the styling, again similar to the D-Type Jaguar, was handled by Clare MacKichan, who was head of the Chevrolet styling section. About the only familiar production part in the SS was the 283-cubic-inch V-8 with fuel injection. But that too benefited from special intake and exhaust manifolds and aluminium cylinder heads to produce 307 horsepower.

Though the effort to prepare the SS for Sebring was intense and had high-level authority, the work on the race car went on around other projects. So there was actually little time to bring all aspects together in a race-ready vehicle. Initial plans had been to build four Corvette SS models, but lack of time cut that to one. As Sebring, which is held in early spring, loomed, a test version of the SS, called a mule, was readied for suspension and brake testing. It had a crude white fiberglass body and a less powerful V-8, though the suspension was identical to the finished SS chassis.

With Sebring just days away, it became apparent to outside observers that the Corvette SS was going to make the green flag with only hours to spare. As workers in Michigan hurried to finish the SS, Duntov took the mule vehicle to Sebring for last-minute testing and driver practice.

Initially, in keeping with the high hopes Chevrolet had for the Corvette SS, Stirling Moss and Juan Fangio were signed to drive. But as doubts arose over whether Chevrolet would make the race, both superstars accepted other rides. An effort was made to get Carroll Shelby, but he too eventually declined. In the end, John Fitch and Italian driver Piero Taruffi were secured as the driving team. Although they were no longer on the team, Moss and Fangio did take a few spins on the mule version of the SS.

The results were astounding. Although it was heavier and less powerful than the refined SS, Fangio unofficially broke the Sebring lap record in the car.

But things were not to be that simple once the finished Corvette SS, looking stunning in its blue paint with brushed metal accents, arrived by truck from Detroit. Bob Cumberford, who worked on the SS design, was a member of the pit crew and he recalls that concern over making sure the Corvette SS looked good cosmetically helped doom the Sebring effort. 'Once the car got to Sebring, Harley Earl limited the amount of practice in the car because he didn't want it to get any chips or dings before the race,' he comments. 'He wanted it to look pretty.'

When the endurance race began with Fitch at the wheel of a largely untested car, the Corvette SS showed its biggest flaw. The magnesium body would not dissipate the under-hood heat generated by the engine and brakes. The result was that the cockpit became a broiler in the hot Florida sun and delicate parts cooked.

'That's why it failed,' says Cumberford, 'because they didn't practice in it, they didn't know about the heat buildup, which, among other things, cooked the rubber suspension bushings.' Fitch fought with the heat for 22 laps before he brought the car into the pits, exhausted. It was not a stellar day for Chevrolet and some tempers were as hot as the car. Ed Cole told Taruffi to take the car out and see what he could do. After one lap, Taruffi brought the car back and supported Fitch's assessment.

As disastrous as Sebring was for the Corvette team, no one at the time thought it would be the last effort at international sports car racing. Cole issued orders that the shortcomings of the Corvette SS were to be fixed and an improved version readied for the 24-hour race at Le Mans.

Before that plan could be put into effect, the top brass at General Motors, never wholly at ease with this racing business, squashed Team Corvette.

The event that was the flashpoint for the abrupt turn away from racing came on June 4, 1957, when the Automobile Manufacturer's Association officially banned factory-sponsored racing. Jack Gordon, the new president at GM, was also a member of the national safety council – which was decrying the highway death toll of 50,000 a year – and he was not at all a supporter of auto racing. He decreed that the ban would be fully enforced.

The reason for the ban is a little murky and had much to do with politics. By 1957, Detroit had discovered the use of safety features as a sales tool. Padded dashes and seat belts were in vogue. But so, too, was the trend toward faster and more aggressive cars. Many in the US automobile business feared that the federal government would step in and slap regulations on Detroit if the 'Big Three' did not act responsibly. Perhaps the biggest splash Detroit could make was to ban its participation in auto racing. It was an action that didn't cost any dollars – unlike a

commitment to actually make production cars safer – and in fact it probably saved a few bucks.

As with most political decisions, the ban on racing was not all that it appeared to be. Many people within Ford, Chrysler and Chevrolet knew that a significant number of car buyers wanted their cars to be faster and better handling. Those same people also wanted to be able to see a link between their passenger cars and exotic race cars. So the participation of Detroit in racing was continued through indirect means, such as the sponsorship of private teams and the creation of 'special products' divisions. But Chevrolet was far more secretive about its racing effort, particularly where the Corvette was concerned.

The most successful Corvette racer of the 1950s was Dick Thompson, who was a Washington, DC, dentist weekdays and a very talented race driver on weekends. Starting in 1956, he and his Corvettes dominated the B Production class in SCCA racing for years.

BELOW *Brakes had been a problem on the SS, were a problem on the Sting Ray, and were constantly criticized by the individual Corvette weekend racers. RPO 686, as fitted to this '61, was the answer. In 686, sintered-metallic linings acted upon highly polished unfinned drums, to satisfy the owner who wanted braking strength for competition, allied to smooth performance without pulling and chattering, on the street.*

Publicly, GM was adamant about its involvement in racing: there was none. People like Thompson were just accomplished amateurs racing a very good Chevrolet product, just like the car anyone can buy at their local dealer. But there is ample evidence that was just not the case.

Cumberford recalls that it was well-known among workers at GM that Thompson and others received some factory help. But few knew how extensive that help was. 'I went into the Chevrolet garage with Ed Cole one day and walking across the garage I spotted three red Corvettes sitting there,' Cumberford says. 'Cole got distracted and I looked more closely at the cars.

'I had a wonderful photograph of Dick Thompson leading the field at Pebble Beach past the pits and the California license plate on the car was BXL 190. Every time I drew a Corvette – had a new design idea – that's the license number I would put on it. So I had the number of Thompson's car memorized.

'What caught my eye that day in the garage with Cole was that all three of those red Corvettes were identical to Thompson's car and all three had BXL 190 plates on the front. Now, two of the cars could have those plates on the front because the states issues two plates, a front and a rear. But three of them was a little hard to believe,' he remembers.

'So when Cole was distracted I went and looked at the cars. The plates were obviously counterfeits. A license plate has stamped into it a serial number other than the registration number and it was the same on all three plates. So there were three identical cars and if you look at where Dick Thompson was racing, in Florida one week and then Bellingham, Washington, another and then Watkins Glen, New York, later on, there was always a red Corvette there with BXL plates. It was clearly an expensive and well-planned effort by GM.'

Whether it was through covert operations at Chevrolet or through the dint of hard work by genuine independent racers, the Corvette

was starting to make its mark by the late 1950s.

Starting with its first B production national title in 1957, the Corvette dominated that category up until 1963, when the lighter and, arguably, less-production oriented Cobra made its debut.

Many race drivers cut their teeth on Corvettes and went on to success in other forms of racing. One of those was Bob Bondurant, who now runs perhaps the most famous driving school in the world, the 'Bob Bondurant School of High-Performance Driving' at Sears Point Raceway near San Francisco.

Bondurant says that by the late 1950s, the Corvette was a mainstay of SCCA racing. 'You'd have fields with 30 to 35 Corvettes racing at one time,' he says. 'That was almost the feature race at that time.'

Bondurant's first ride in a competition Corvette came at Pebble Beach in 1958, when he bought a '57 Vette from Jerry Austin, who had taken West Coast B Production honors in the car the year before. 'When I bought that '57 it was really competitive,' Bondurant recalls. 'My first race I finished third. I was amazed at how well it went.' Talk of the Corvette being an ill-mannered car on the track was just plain wrong, he says. 'The rap against the early Corvettes was unfair. What happened is you'd have cars like the Mercedes 300 SL, the Jags and things like that winning the races. And then this fiberglass-bodied car from the States came out and started beating them or almost beating them. Then in '57, the Corvettes started winning all the races.'

Bondurant remembers that the solid-axle Corvettes required a very aggressive driving style. 'At that time you drove the Corvette sideways,' he says. 'It had skinny little tires on

Bob Bondurant's Sting Ray with the ZO6 competition package first raced on October 13, 1962, at the Los Angeles Times Three-Hour Invitational at Riverside. Alongside him were three other ZO6 option Sting Rays, one of which, driven by Doug Hooper, took the checkered flag. The race also saw the debut of Carroll Shelby's awesome Ford-powered Cobra, which would dominate production-class racing for the rest of the decade.

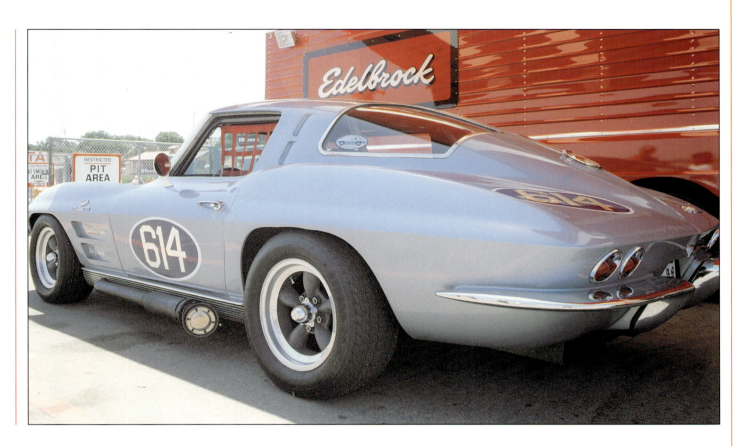

ABOVE *Racer Vic Edelbrock's ZO6 Sting Ray; the ZO6 Special Performance Equipment package provided stiffer springs, a bigger anti-roll bar, a 36-gallon fiberglass fuel tank (coupe only) vented heavy-duty brakes, the strongest fuel-injected engine available, and was, not surprisingly, very expensive.*

it and lots of horsepower. It was very, very responsive. The brakes were good – it had drum brakes and sintered-metallic linings. You had to heat them up a little before they would work, but the hotter you got them the better they worked.'

As Bondurant became more successful, he began to benefit from the unofficial help Chevrolet was handing out to Corvette racers. 'Chevrolet wasn't in racing, yet they were in racing out the back door,' he explains. 'I didn't have any sponsorship – I wish I had. We paid for our own racing in those days and then I finally got a sponsor in '59 and we won 18 out of 20 races.

'Once I won that many races and the West Coast B Production Championship, then all of a sudden the motor arrived and a special gearbox arrived in a crate and some things just sort of showed up from Chevrolet.

Nothing was ever said about it, you just got it and did it.'

Bondurant was in on the beginning of the Corvette's first reign in racing and he was there also for the end of that era in 1963. When the new Sting Ray appeared for the '63 model year, Chevrolet offered an option with the order code Z06. Checking the Z06 box caused the factory to crank out a Corvette that was ready for racing. Stuffed under the standard Sting Ray exterior were heavy-duty springs, a larger anti-roll bar, a 36-gallon fiberglass fuel tank, beefier disc brakes and the 360-horsepower 327 fuel-injection engine.

Bondurant was one of the first people to drive a Z06 Corvette. An old sponsor, Washburn Chevrolet in Santa Barbara, California, called Bondurant and said there was one waiting for him at the factory. Before the Washburn offer came through, Bondurant was being courted by Carroll Shelby to drive his new car, the Cobra. 'I remember Carroll Shelby asked me to drive the Cobra and he was going to have one ready for Santa Barbara, and it wasn't ready. And then it was going to be ready for Pomona, and it wasn't ready, and I thought, "Well, he doesn't have any money and he's not going to get it done," comments Bondurant.

So with no Cobra in hand, Bondurant and two other Corvette racers, David MacDonald and Jerry Grant, flew to St. Louis, took delivery of three Z06 Sting Rays and drove them back to the West Coast. Bondurant saw

immediately that the Sting Ray was a much better race car than the solid-axle Corvette. 'The car handled better, the brakes were better and there was a little more power,' he says. 'You could get all the power to the ground and the whole thing really worked well. It was a very easy car to drive.'

Bondurant and the school of Sting Rays made their debut at the Los Angeles Times Grand Prix at Riverside Raceway.

Bill Mitchell's Sting Ray must be one of the most attractive cars ever to have graced a race track. It always ran in the 1957 chassis, but two changes in 1960 made it truly competitive: the heavy GRP body was replaced with a better finished version weighing 75 pounds less, and the old and unreliable SS brakes were replaced with a simpler, more durable system.

ABOVE *Except for that first victory at Riverside in 1962, Z06 one/Cobra two was not the norm. The Cobra, after all, had been designed solely to win races – the Sting Ray was a legitimate street car with a roof and reasonable interior space.*

RIGHT *Zora Arkus-Duntov's Grand Sport, Chevy's last "officially" supported factory competition car, and Duntov's reply to the Shelby Cobra.*

Unfortunately, Shelby had finally gotten his Cobra together for the same race. 'Billy Krause drove the first Cobra at Riverside when we drove the first Sting Rays and he ran off and hid from us until he broke a half-shaft,' Bondurant recalls. 'Corvettes finished one, two, three, and four, but the handwriting was sort of on the wall. David MacDonald left the Corvettes to drive for Shelby and he would just blow us off. We could stay with him in the turns – we were quicker in the corners – but he could out-brake us and out-accelerate because the Cobra was lighter. I was the only Corvette Sting Ray that could stay with the Cobra, but I could never beat them.'

In August of 1963, Bondurant too switched over to the Cobra team. But he still remembers those early Corvettes as champions: 'I really pretty much made my name in Corvettes. The Corvette was a fun car to drive and it handled well. It was really a good car.'

The arrival of the Cobra, with its full support from Ford, didn't sit at all well with Duntov and others who loved the Corvette. But there was the problem of the GM policy against factory race cars. Although Ford and Chrysler quietly abandoned the stance in 1962 and resumed above-board racing, GM clung to the ban. Even though the unacknowledged efforts to help private teams continued, Duntov and others knew it would take a factory effort to make the Corvette number one.

Toward the end, Duntov and Semon E 'Bunkie' Knudsen, the new boss at Chevrolet, decided to push the corporate edict and see how far they could get. The goal was to build a Corvette to compete for the FIA world championship against Ferrari and the new Cobra. Under changed rules, specially equipped GT cars could compete for the championship provided at least 100 such cars had been produced for public consumption. Duntov saw an opportunity and started to design the ultimate racing Sting Ray. Operating on the theory that they would do what was necessary until someone from above said stop, Knudsen signed off on a plan to build 125 Grand Sport Corvettes.

The Grand Sport that Duntov constructed looked like a Corvette, but that's where the similarity stopped. The Grand Sport was designed around a ladder-type frame

constructed of tubular steel. The new independent rear suspension received larger half-shafts and a lighter leaf spring was installed. The steering was modified and the mechanical components lightened. Outboard four-wheel disc brakes were used.

The body was fiberglass, but it was much thinner and lighter than the stock shell. An aluminum birdcage was installed and the disappearing headlights jettisoned in favor of fixed lights under plexiglass covers. In finished form, the Grand Sport would weigh just 2,000 lb.

For power, Duntov pulled out all the stops. He envisioned an all-aluminium version of the 327 fuel-injection engine that would, at the limits, displace 402 cubic inches. Using twin-plug hemispherical cylinder heads, the monster engine would produce 600 horsepower. To start, the engine would be

enlarged to 377 cubic inches and produce 550 horsepower.

The Duntov-Knudson plan to test the limits of corporate tolerance was a good one. Unfortunately, they found out just what those limits were. Gm's then chief executive, Frederic Donner, blew a gasket when he found out about the Grand Sport project. He sent word that engaging in corporate-sponsored racing was a firing offense and the Grand Sport project was stopped.

Although the monster hemi-head engine was never produced, Duntov had enough parts to cobble together five Grand Sports. In the interest of maximizing corporate assets, these were sold off to private racers who

ABOVE *Duntov had plans for modifying the standard 327 for use in the Grand Sport, by adding hemispherical combustion chambers and two plugs per cylinder, to produce a staggering 600 bhp.*

Once again, the AMA racing edict interfered, and he had to settle for a not unrespectable 377-cid four Weber carburetor powerplant, producing 485 bhp for the Nassau showdown with Shelby.

TOP AND ABOVE RIGHT *Grand Sports can still be seen in vintage racing; all five originally produced still exist in good condition.*

campaigned them with disappointing results, given the lack of factory help. The Cobras trounced the Corvettes in 1963.

Always a proud man, Duntov rankled under the defeats the Cobras were handing out. He and Knudsen decided to test the corporate edict one last time. Two Grand Sports were repossessed and a third was built by Chevrolet Engineering. The front man for this operation was Texan John Mecom and the

goal was to carve up the Cobras at the racing season finale at Nassau in the Bahamas. When Mecom's Corvettes were delivered to Nassau in late December in '63, there was no doubt about why they were there.

The three Grand Sports were equipped with all-aluminum 377 cubic-inch V-8s that were topped with Weber carburetors. More

than 485 horsepower was on tap, and the Grand Sports throttled the Cobras. Though the Chevy conspirators escaped with their jobs, the final word from the GM boardroom was succinct. Get rid of the Grand Sports and behave yourselves. It would be six years before Corvettes again resumed their domination of American sports car racing.

TOP *The GT-40 from Ford, seen here between two Grand Sports, would finally spell the end for front-engined sports/racers.*

ABOVE AND BELOW LEFT *Grand Sport #003, lent by Engineering to Dick Doane to race when GM stuck to the AMA racing ban in 1963, is now owned by Robert Paterson.*

FROM SPORTS CAR TO MUSCULAR DRAGSTER

W hen the job of designing an all-new Corvette came around, there was a changing of the guard at General Motors. Harley Earl, the iron-willed leader of the GM Styling Studio, retired in 1959 and left behind as his successor William Leroy Mitchell.

Where Earl often accomplished great things through sheer willpower, Mitchell, known to all as Bill, was a man who moved people through enthusiasm and creativity. He began sketching cars in his youth and, while an illustrator at the Barron Collier Advertising Agency in the early 1930s, attended the Art Student's League in New York. His love of cars was a legacy from his

BELOW *Bill Mitchell used the Sting Ray racer as a runabout in the mid-1960s, with a new paint job – and disc brakes, something the Corvette had needed as far back as the SS.*

father, who was a Buick dealer in Pennsylvania.

Mitchell was fascinated by the English sports cars of the time, Rileys and MGs. Along with the sons of Barron Collier, he held impromptu sports car races. He was eventually one of the founders of the American Racing Car Association, which later became the Sports Car Club of America.

Mitchell's opportunity to put his love of cars to work came in December of 1935 when he joined General Motors' Art and Color Section as a designer. A friend of Earl's had spotted some of Mitchell's work at Collier's and put the two men together, and they hit it off.

Their passion for automotive design and their respect for each other's work helped bridge the differences in style between the two men. Working under Earl, Mitchell was able to create some significant designs, starting with the Cadillac 60 Special in 1938.

By the time Earl was ready to step down in 1959, Mitchell was ready to leave his own mark on GM products. Building on the considerable power left to him by Earl, Mitchell combined showmanship, support for his staff's designs and the courage to take a stand in the face of widespread corporate disagreement.

Corvette was fortunate to have someone such as Mitchell in charge of its metamorphosis. The car that Mitchell set to work refurbishing had come a long way from the Motorama car created by Earl. It was powerful and a proven race track winner. Sales were steadily on the rise, though still miniscule compared to overall GM sales.

But there was lots of room for improvement. The chassis of the Corvette, though updated, was still the same basic layout that could have been found under any Chevrolet, circa 1953. And the body, once a 'dream car' shape, was now looking quite dated, especially when compared to the upcoming XKE Jaguar.

Mitchell's love of the sports car was evident. In an interview with *Automobile Quarterly,* Mitchell said this of designing a sports car: 'You know, the great thing about a sports car, that size of car, is that when you've designed the thing, you can put your arms around it. You can't do that with a passenger car. You can really enjoy the form.' Like Zora Arkus-Duntov, the Corvette's chief engineer, Mitchell believed in the value of race-bred automobiles. The first hint of what the next generation Corvette would look like began life as Mitchell's personal race car.

As discussed elsewhere, GM's strict adherence to the Automobile Manufacturers Association ban on racing cut down a fledgling effort at international sports car racing. One of the leftovers from that aborted effort was the test bed, or mule car, for the Corvette SS.

Relegated to the corner in some GM garage, Mitchell saw the mule chassis as a perfect platform for his own Corvette creation. The only problem was to somehow circumvent the corporate racing ban. With the help of Ed Cole, head of Chevrolet, Mitchell bought the mule chassis for one dollar and an official agreement that the car would be a hobby vehicle for Mitchell. As with other racing situations at GM through the years, the above-board deal was considerably different from reality.

Keeping the mule chassis pretty much as it was when it lapped Sebring, Mitchell worked with a team of GM designers, including Larry Shinoda, to create the car's new body. What emerged in 1959 from a secret studio was a breakthrough concept. Looking almost like an airfoil, the rebodied Sebring mule was one of the most beautiful cars of its time. Low and with taut lines, the most impressive features were the sexy fender bulges at the wheel wells, the wrap-around windscreen and the pointed power bulge on the hood.

It is a testament to Mitchell's abilities, not only as a designer but also as a corporate salesman, that much of the flavor of his race car, dubbed the Sting Ray, was retained in the 1963 production car.

Though exciting to look at, the Sting Ray racer was less than successful at the track. The lower body panels, which curved under to give an appearance of hugging the road, did exactly the opposite, causing the car to lift at speed. Also, the mule chassis still suffered from many of the vices that plagued the Corvette SS, most notably quirky brakes.

Still, with the Corvette's corporate racer at the helm, Dr Dick Thompson, the Sting Ray eventually was made to behave. By 1960 the car managed to win top C-Modified Production honors in SCCA racing, though it never visited the winner's circle. With a pedigree of sorts, the Sting Ray was acknowledged by GM and, with the name Corvette added to its flanks, it was put on the show car tour.

BELOW RIGHT *The famous divided back light on the 1963 Sting Ray; it was cancelled after one year, making this a highly sought-after collectible today. The design of the humped fenders owes much to the Sting Ray racer.*

The design themes for the 1963 Corvette were also tested in a few other show cars, including the XP-700, which featured the ducktail rear end that appeared on the 1961 Corvette, and the Corvette Shark, inspired by a catch Mitchell made on a fishing expedition.

What did not publicly appear until the '63 Corvette's introduction was the coupe version, which sported the controversial 'split window' design. Mitchell was in love with the shape of the coupe's rear flow, which had a wind split line running from the top to the rear deck. It traversed the rear window via a thick metal divider.

Duntov and Mitchell could never see eye-to-eye on the split window design. Duntov thought it was a needless bit of form over function that obscured the driver's rear vision. Mitchell defended it as a crucial part of the coupe's overall styling. He won the battle, and the split window debuted on the production car. But Duntov won the war: the bar was removed after the '63 model.

The other aspect of the new Corvette that added to its racy appearance was its concealed headlights. Not a new idea – cars such as the Cord 812 had them in the 1930s – the flip-up lights smoothed out the Corvette's design. To make them work, the nose of the car had to be made slightly wider than on the prototype to accommodate the electric motors that opened the lights.

Its styling assets aside, the people who worked with Duntov in engineering the new Corvette were no less creative than Mitchell's designers. Having introduced the new 327-cubic-inch V8 on the '62 Corvette, Chevrolet engineers concentrated on making the new Corvette handle. The biggest step in that direction came with the addition of independent rear suspension.

The biggest handling drawback on the original Corvette was its solid rear axle. On uneven surfaces and in cornering, the solid axle demanded that both wheels act in unison. That created skittish behaviour. With independent suspension, each wheel can deal with changing road and handling conditions. Also, because the independent suspension distributes the car's weight better, vehicle ride quality is improved. In designing the new Corvette's rear suspension, Duntov and company created a system that used a combination of half-shafts, trailing arms and a transverse leaf spring assembly.

The independent suspension was mounted in a new Corvette frame that replaced the X-type setup on the original Vette. Based on a shorter 98-inch wheelbase, the new Corvette

BELOW The public took to the aggressive looks of the new Corvette immediately; one of the few (occasional) complaints was about the use of dummy vents on the coupe's rear pillars.

frame was a ladder design that used boxed rails and five crossmembers. The new frame allowed the body to be mounted lower, thus substantially decreasing the car's center of gravity.

Thanks to a shift in the engine's mounting position, the front/rear balance on the new Corvette worked out to 49 per cent front/ 50 per cent rear – a theoretically perfect arrangement.

So with the improved engine-transmission assembly from the '62 Corvette in place, the '63 Corvette proved to be a substantially superior car to its predecessors. Handling was sharply improved, there was a better ride, there was more interior room and, thanks to the rear suspension, the Corvette was also faster.

C O R V E T T E S H O W D O W N		
	1963 CORVETTE	**1963 JAGUAR XKE**
Price	$4,037	$5,600
Dimensions		
Wheelbase (inches)	102	96
Length (inches)	175.3	175
Weight (pounds)	3,030	2,690
Engine and Drivetrain type	Fuel-injected V-8	Overhead Camshaft Six
Displacement (c.i.)	327	231
Horsepower	360	265
Transmission	Four-speed manual	Four-speed manual
Performance		
0–60 mph	5.9 seconds	7.1 seconds
Top Speed	142 mph	149 mph

To say that the new Corvette was a hit with buyers would be an understatement. The '62 Corvette enjoyed the best sales year in Corvette history, with 14,531 cars out the door. The '63 Corvette would shatter that mark, with more than 21,500 cars being sold at a record base price of more than $4,000. In its October, 1962, edition, *Road & Track* had high praise for the new Corvette: 'As a purely sporting car, the new Corvette will know few peers on road or track . . . in its nice, shiny new concept, it ought to be nearly unbeatable.'

The praise was well deserved, since a street Corvette was capable of performance on a par with the world's best sports cars.

Equipped with the 360-horsepower fuel-injection engine, the '63 Corvette could hit 143 mph, and sprint to 60 mph in 5.9 seconds.

Though the arrival of Carroll Shelby's Cobra spoiled the Corvette's race track debut, there's no doubt that the Cobra was less of a street car than the Corvette. Buyers of a Corvette could choose from an option list that included airconditioning, power steering, power brakes, power windows and leather seats. The Cobra was brawnier, but the Corvette was better suited for trips to the grocery store.

So perfect was the '63 Corvette that the arrival of the '64 showed few changes. The rear window bar on the coupe was gone – though today the split-window Corvette is a coveted item – and minor refinements were made to the dash. Engine power hit an all-time high, with the fuel-injection 327 being rated at 375 horsepower. Sales continued to climb, with more than 22,000 cars bought.

Despite all these bright spots – and the undeniable fact that the 327-cubic-inch Corvette was one of the world's best balanced sports cars – many of Corvette's boosters and detractors continued to see one glaring problem: quality control.

The Corvette had long had a reputation as a car with lots of rattles, leaks and rough workmanship. Most people felt that a car costing more than $4,000 should be better put

CORVETTE SHOWDOWN		
	1964 CORVETTE	**1964 289 COBRA**
Price	$4,463	$5,995
Dimensions		
Wheelbase (inches)	98	90
Length (inches)	175.1	151.5
Weight (pounds)	3,430	2,540
Engine and Drivetrain type	Fuel-injected V-8	Carbureted V-8
Displacement (c.i.)	327	289
Horsepower	375	271
Transmission	Four-speed manual	Four-speed manual
Performance		
0–60 mph	6.3 seconds	6.6 seconds
Top Speed	138 mph	139 mph

together. Some of the problems can be traced to the fact that the Corvette was an assembly-line automobile, while its competitors, such as Porsche, Jaguar and Ferrari, were nearly hand-built by comparison, if not in reality. The rest of the problem could be squarely placed at the doormat of the local Chevy dealer. Though some dealers made an effort to cater to Corvette buyers, most treated the Corvette as if it was just a two-seat Impala.

Ron Wakefield, a writer for *Road & Track*, recounted in the magazine's February, 1967, edition the problems he had when he bought a new '64 Corvette: 'The car was delivered to me with no more than a wash job, apparently. Problems: a broken spark plug; the side windows wouldn't roll up with the doors shut; splotchy paint on top cover panel; the top didn't fit properly; the passenger's seat rattled furiously; leaks around the windshield; and the steering had a massive squeak in it.

'Details of the experience of getting these faults corrected approach the sordid and don't bear going into here; since then I've come to the conclusion that the condition of my car was typical and the dealer service was typical. In my experience it seems most Chevrolet dealers look upon the Corvette as some kind of Funny Furrin Car.'

That the Corvette was so popular with buyers is a tribute to the car's nature. Imagine how well the early Corvettes would have done with a little TLC from the factory and the dealers. It would be nearly 20 years before the issue of quality control on the Corvette would be addressed.

The arrival of the '65 Corvette signaled the car's entry into the horsepower wars that would consume Detroit in the latter half of the 1960s. Long a proponent of the virtues of a Corvette that didn't sacrifice balance for speed, Duntov had shied away from stuffing the big-block Chevrolet engine into the Vette.

But by '65, the Corvette's position as the American car on the cutting edge of performance was being eroded. Cars such as the Pontiac GTO, the Oldsmobile 442 and the Chevelle 396 were winning the stoplight grand prix. Ford had its 427 cubic-inch V-8 and Chrysler had the monster 426 Hemi engine. The 327, a game little engine, had gone as far as it could go.

It is a Detroit adage that there is no substitute for cubic inches, and that maxim was applied to the Corvette in 1965. An option on that year's car was the 396-cubic-inch V-8, dubbed the 'porcupine' due to the design of its valve train. The valves were canted in the cylinder head, causing the valve stems to stick out like porcupine quills.

Using a single Holley four-barrel carburetor, the Corvette version of this engine pumped out 425 horsepower. Though the 375-horsepower fuel-injection small block engine was still available, it was more expensive and its days were numbered. The larger engine added 150 pounds over the front wheels, but the Corvette suspension handled it with very few complaints.

A necessary styling change for the big-block cars was a power bulge on the hood, which allowed the air cleaner on the 396 to clear the hood. Also, function side vents were added to expel the added engine heat.

Two other important changes were made to the '65 Corvette, one largely cosmetic, the other a Godsend. Side exhausts, long featured on Corvette show cars, became a production item. Buyers loved the way they looked and sounded, though they did result in some singed socks. A more rational addition was the introduction of four-wheel disc brakes.

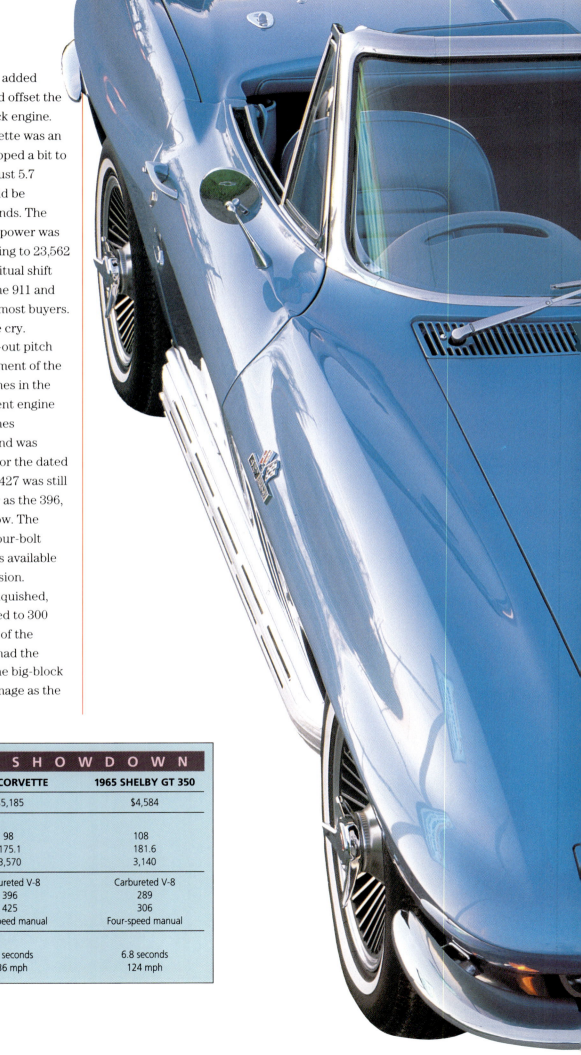

Though not planned together, the added stopping power of the discs helped offset the new forward thrust of the big-block engine.

Overall, the '65 big-block Corvette was an awesome package. Top speed dropped a bit to 136 mph, but 60 mph came up in just 5.7 seconds and the quarter-mile could be covered in a tick less than 14 seconds. The decision to go for maximum horsepower was approved by buyers, with sales rising to 23,562 cars that year. The Corvette's spiritual shift away from such cars as the Porsche 911 and the XKE Jaguar was irrelevant to most buyers. Higher straight-line speed was the cry.

In 1966, Chevrolet made an all-out pitch for power and upped the displacement of the big-block engine to 427-cubic-inches in the Corvette. Two versions of the potent engine were offered. One of the 427 engines produced 'only' 390 horsepower and was available with either a four-speed or the dated two-speed Powerglide. The other 427 was still rated at the same 425 horsepower as the 396, though that figure was probably low. The higher output engine came with four-bolt bearing caps for reliability and was available only tied to a four-speed transmission.

The fuel-injection 327 was vanquished, and the standard 327 was upgraded to 300 horsepower. Though the majority of the 27,720 Corvettes delivered in '66 had the small-block engine, the allure of the big-block 427 was important to Corvette's image as the meanest car on the street.

CORVETTE SHOWDOWN

	1965 CORVETTE	1965 SHELBY GT 350
Price	$5,185	$4,584
Dimensions		
Wheelbase (inches)	98	108
Length (inches)	175.1	181.6
Weight (pounds)	3,570	3,140
Engine and Drivetrain type	Carbureted V-8	Carbureted V-8
Displacement (c.i.)	396	289
Horsepower	425	306
Transmission	Four-speed manual	Four-speed manual
Performance		
0–60 mph	5.7 seconds	6.8 seconds
Top Speed	136 mph	124 mph

So critical was the big-block engine that in 1967 Chevrolet offered four versions in the Corvette. There was the base 427, with a cast-iron intake manifold and a single four-barrel carburetor. Then there were two versions of the 427 that were topped with three two-barrel carburetors. One version offered 400 horsepower, while the other, through the use of aluminium cylinder heads, pumped out 435 horsepower. Heat was a factor with most of the big-block cars and the 435-horsepower version also suffered from warping of the aluminium cylinder heads.

The 1966 Sting Ray Roadster; listed at $4,084, 17,762 were built.

*The main differences between the 1965 model **FAR LEFT** and the style for 1966, were the 1966 B-pillar, and changes to the grille.*

TOP LEFT *The 1966 Mark IV 427 engine: 0–60 in five seconds, top speed in excess of 140 mph.*

LEFT CENTER *"427 Turbo-Jet"; the badging indicates the existence under the hood bulge of the 396 engine bored out to 4.25 inches, offering 50 extra lbs/ft of torque – 365 at 3600 rpm.*

LEFT *The "twin cowl" cockpit of the 1966 Sting Ray.*

The fourth version of the 427 that was available was known by its order code, L-88. This engine existed as another way for Chevrolet to get back-door help to racers without violating GM's anti-racing edict. So potent was the L-88 engine that Chevy advised dealers to discourage customers from ordering it.

Rated at a conservative 430 horsepower – it was actually good for something approaching 550 horsepower – the L-88 was unfit for street use. It used a huge 850-cfm Holley carburetor, a wild camshaft and 12.5–to–1 aluminium cylinder heads. To get one, a buyer had to delete the interior heater. Fewer than two dozen L-88s were delivered in 1967 – that figure would jump to more than

100 in 1968 – and today they are the most coveted of collector Corvettes.

Despite all the added horsepower options in '67, the Corvette saw sales slip to fewer than 23,000 as people anticipated the redesigned '68 Sting Ray. Although it was in production only five years, Bill Mitchell's Sting Ray had traveled quite a few miles. In 1963, the Corvette was striving to be the well-balanced, nimble sports car that Harley Earl hoped for back in 1953. By 1967, it was a brute of a car that thrilled buyers with its tire-ripping acceleration.

The arrival of Mitchell's new Corvette design in '68 would give the buying public a shape that matched the Vette's new-found muscular image.

THE ENDURING STINGRAY

As exciting as the Sting Ray design was in 1963, the car that was to follow it in 1968 would stand as one of the most radical street car designs ever to come out of Detroit. The '68 design was so bold and fresh that it would remain in production for more than 14 years – a miracle in Detroit, where designs change every three years on average.

In coming up with a replacement for the '63 Sting Ray, GM design chief Bill Mitchell faced a daunting task. His earlier design was popular with Corvette buyers and was a tribute to his talent. It was a tough act to follow, but the job was a bit easier.

When Mitchell created his first Corvette design, he was working his way out of the shadow of his mentor, Harley Earl, and establishing his power base within GM. Though the '63 design was a revelation when compared to the '53 Corvette, it was within

BELOW AND RIGHT *The link between the new body style for 1968 (right) and the Mako Shark II (below) penned by Larry Shinoda in 1965, is obvious.*

the parameters of mainstream automotive design.

By the time he was to start work on the car that would become the '68 Corvette, Mitchell was a recognized star at GM. In addition to his Sting Ray design, Mitchell's Buick Riviera was also getting rave reviews, as was most all of the GM line-up.

So when it came to a new Corvette, Mitchell had things pretty much his way. John Schinella was a young designer working at GM when the orders for a new Corvette came down. He recalls that there was a certain

magic surrounding Mitchell and that it spilled onto the Corvette.

'Bill Mitchell was an exciting guy,' says Schinella, who now heads GM's California design studio. 'He loved cars, you could just tell. When he came into the studio he would leave a puddle of gasoline on the floor when he left. Mitchell was just a car nut. He had a great vision when it came to the Corvette. He wanted this to be the very best in American design. He did not want it to be what the rest of the world was doing. We weren't out to copy other people. That was

the kind of excitement that prevailed around Bill.'

Larry Shinoda, Schinella and some other designers, including George Angersbach, whose forte was interior design, were given a small, private studio to work on new Corvette creations.

'We came up with a couple of schemes,' remembers Schinella. 'One of them as a mid-engined Corvette. Of course the powers that be were not interested in a mid-engine car. But we did a mid-engine design and the next year Ford came out with their GT 40 and it's

ABOVE *Mako Shark II was reskinned for the 1969 auto show circuit, and renamed the Manta Ray.*

TOP *The original Shark, Bill Mitchell's XP-755 of 1961, later retitled Mako Shark I, had influenced the 1963–1967 Sting Ray, just as the Mako Shark II affected the 1968 redesign.*

amazing how close those two cars were. Great minds think alike.' It was to take nearly 20 years before Schinella and others could convince GM to produce a mid-engine two-seat car – the Pontiac Fiero.

As a measure of the sort of work going on backstage at GM while the design for the '68 Corvette was germinating, Schinella says that interspersed with his Vette duties, he also worked on the design and development of Jim Hall's famed Chapparal race cars. So much for GM's no-racing stance.

RPO #	DESCRIPTION	RETAIL
—	Genuine Leather Seat Trim	$ 79.00
A01	Soft Ray Tinted Glass, All Windows	15.80
A31	Electric Power Windows	57.95
A82	Head Restraints	42.15
A85	Custom Shoulder Belts	26.35
C07	Auxiliary Hardtop (Roadster only)	231.75
C08	Vinyl Covering for Auxiliary Hardtop	52.70
C50	Rear Window Defroster	31.60
C60	Air Conditioning	412.90
F41	Special Front and Rear Suspension	36.90
G81	Positraction Rear Axle (all ratios)	46.35
J50	Power Brakes	42.15
J56	Heavy Duty Brakes	384.45
K66	Transistor Ignition	73.75
L79	Optional 350hp, 327 ci Engine	105.35
L36	Optional 390hp, 427 ci Engine	200.15
L68	Optional 400hp, 427 ci Engine	305.50
L71	Optional 435hp, 427 ci Engine	437.10
L88	Optional 435hp, 427 ci Engine	947.90
L71/89	Optional 435hp, 427 ci Engine	805.75
M20	4-Speed Transmission	184.35
M21	4-Speed Close Ratio Transmission	184.35
M22	4-Speed Close Ratio Transmission, Heavy Duty	263.30
M40	Turbo Hydra-Matic Automatic Transmission	226.45
N11	Off-Road Exhaust System	36.90
N36	Telescopic Steering Column	42.15
N40	Power Steering	94.80
P01	Bright Metal Wheel Covers	57.95
PT6	Red Stripe Nylon Tires, F70/15	31.30
PT7	White Stripe Nylon Tires, F70/15	31.30
UA6	Alarm System	26.35
U15	Speed Warning Indicator	10.55
U69	AM-FM Radio	172.75
U79	AM-FM Stereo Radio	278.10

1968 COLORS

CODE	EXTERIOR	SOFT TOP	WHEELS	SUGGESTED GM INTERIORS
900	Tuxedo Black	Blk-W-Bge	Silver	Blk-R-MB-DB
972	Polar White	Blk-W-Bge	Silver	DO-Tob-Gun
992	Corvette Bronze	Blk-W-Bge	Silver	Blk-DO-Tob
976	LeMans Blue	Blk-W-Bge	Silver	Blk-MB-DB
978	International Blue	Blk-W-Bge	Silver	Blk-MB-DB
988	Cordovan Maroon	Blk-W-Bge	Silver	Blk
974	Rally Red	Blk-W-Bge	Silver	Blk-R
986	Silverstone Silver	Blk-W-Bge	Silver	Blk-DB-Gun
983	British Green	Blk-W-Bge	Silver	Blk
982	Safari Yellow	Blk-W-Bge	Silver	Blk

Interior Codes: Blk/V = Std; Blk/L = 402; R/V = 407; R/L = 408; MB/V = 414; MB/L = 415; DB/V = 411; DO/V = 425; DO/L = 426; Tob/V = 435; Tob/L = 436; Gun/V = 422

Abbreviations: Blk = Black, R = Red, MB = Medium Blue, DB = Dark Blue, DO = Dark Orange, Gun = Gunmetal, W = White, Bge = Beige, Tob = Tobacco, L = Leather, V = Vinyl

Out of this rich atmosphere of ideas and gambles, Shinoda and Schinella distilled the 1965 prototype show car called the Mako Shark II. Although there have been bolder show cars, no GM car destined for production has ever started from such a wild premise.

The primary design cue for the Mako was its flaired pontoon fenders. The large humps over each wheel gave the car the look of an animal crouching. The fenders were strictly form over function, however, since the wheels themselves didn't protrude one inch into the exaggerated wheel wells.

ABOVE *Options for 1968; not surprisingly, it was the L88 engine that cost the most, with its aluminum cylinder heads and intake manifold, dual valve springs and special camshaft. 28,000 Corvette buyers ordered the mono radio – only 60 ordered the L88.*

The fenders were the anchor points for the 'Coke bottle' sweep of the rest of the body, which narrowed at the doors. Up front, the nose was V-shaped and without bumpers, and, as with the production Corvette, the pop-up headlights remained. Leading-edge vents appeared at the front of the hood and a massive, twin-domed power bulge rose up in front of the windshield.

At the back was a wild manta ray type tail that came to a point at the end of the rear deck. Innovative but impractical were the brake lights, which were hidden but lifted into view when the brakes were applied. The fastback rear window was buried under louvers, and the coupe had a removable roof panel. The cockpit was as radical as the exterior, with digital instrumentation and a general fighter-jet motif. Many of the gauges were relocated into a binnacle that split the dashboard and ran between the seats. Underneath, the Mako was pretty much a stock '64 Corvette. It was first fitted with the 396 cubic-inch V-8, and later a 427 was put under the hood.

Overall, the Mako Shark II was a stunner when it debuted at the New York auto show in April of 1965. The public loved it, and the Mako Shark would remain a popular show car for several years. But the first storm clouds of criticism from automotive journalists began to appear. Longer, heavier and less graceful, the Mako was not the direction some felt America's sports car design should be heading.

Mitchell, however, felt the Mako was right on target and plans proceeded to introduce the new body style as the 1967 Corvette. As happened with the 1963 split-window coupe, Mitchell's design would run up against the functional concerns of Zora Arkus-Duntov, still the Corvette's chief engineer.

Although Duntov probably would have preferred a lighter, more nimble design for the car, he recognized that flashy designs often sold more cars than well-engineered components. Still, he was adamant about the new Corvette being delayed until his

In addition to the Mako design, Schinella and others also worked on a mockup that would have taken Corvette design down a different road. 'We tried to do one that was more tubular, without the fenders,' Schinella says. 'We made a model that was split down

The flying buttress rear treatment would survive from 1968 to 1977. It was always intended that the backlight as well as that part of the roof above the seats be removable, to combine the open-air appeal of the roadster with the weather protection and greater rigidity of the closed body.

RIGHT *There were dark days ahead for performance machines with tighter emissions controls and then the oil crisis; in 1971, Ed Cole foresaw the mandatory introduction of catalytic converters on US cars – which meant no lead – before it happened. But the new model for 1968 had no such inhibitions.*

objections were dealt with. Primary among Duntov's concerns was the degree to which the fenders obstructed the driver's field of view. The pontoons would have to be reduced in size. There were other serious concerns, such as the addition of bumpers and the redesign of the sensational but wholly impractical rear deck.

Working in a new, separate studio called Chevy II, Schinella was a part of the team that worked on turning the Mako into a real-world automobile. Aside from adding bumpers and toning down the fender flairs and the hood bulges, the big change was at the back. In place of the fastback design, a notchback approach was used with small sails blending into the rear fenders. The rear deck now ended cleanly with a small spoiler lip and a scooped out tail. Viewed from the side, the rear quarter design is very reminiscent of the 1964 Ferrari GTO.

the middle. On one side was the Mako approach, and the other showed the tubular design. We developed both because Mitchell wanted to look at both approaches in design. So we remained flexible right down to the end, when a decision was made to go with the more flamboyant design that had more character.'

When the design was finalized – and Duntov's objections taken care of – it was too late to make the '67 model year, and the new Corvette was introduced as a '68 model. Buyers flocked to dealer showrooms to see the new Vette and the response was almost universally positive. America was on the verge of landing men on the moon and the new Corvette looked like the vehicle they might use to get there.

The absence of vent windows – the script logo 'Astro Ventilation' replaced them – along with other small touches, such as the console instrument pod, flush door handles and a rudimentary fiber-optic exterior light monitorin system, made the Corvette appear very special.

Underneath the new face, much of the '67 running gear was carried over. There was the daunting array of engine power, including the three 427-cubic-inch options. The suspension geometry remained much the same, though

the car rode much more stiffly, thanks to changes in the spring rates.

The biggest mechanical news was the addition of the silky smooth three-speed Turbo Hydramatic transmission. It handled the awesome torque of the Chevy V-8s and gave up little to the manual transmissions.

While the Corvette was a hit with the public, hard-core sports car enthusiasts and the motoring press were underwhelmed. The '68 Corvette continued what they saw as an alarming trend away from a two-seat sports car and toward a plush, two-seat dragster. The new Corvette was guilty of several apparent sins: it was longer by seven inches – all of it hanging ponderously ahead of the front wheels – and it was heavier by nearly 100 pounds.

What the Corvette was also guilty of were a few production glitches that made living with the new car difficult for many owners. Chief among the complaints was the problem of keeping the 427 engines running cool. Many big-blocks were eventually pulled from the cars in later years by owners frustrated with keeping the high-strung engines running. Also, rain leaks were not uncommon, the new door latches often became stuck and the new body was prone to a whole host of new

BELOW *The problem that faced Mitchell and the other designers when it came to the new 1968 Corvette was that the '63–'67 Sting Ray had been so good: to introduce a new design that did not improve on its predecessor would have been disastrous. Inevitably, there were compromises forced upon Mitchell's striving for a radical new look based upon the Mako Shark II. Duntov insisted, for example, that the proposed front fenders be lowered to improve vision.*

squeaks and rattles. And, for all the added dimensions outside, there was less interior and luggage space than in the '67 model.

Still, the new Corvette was a sales success. With the base price pegged at $4,320 – the most Corvettes going out the door at option-laden prices of above $5,000 – 28,566 Vettes were sold in 1968. It was a tribute to the stunning new design that owners were willing to overlook some shortcomings to drive such an attention-getting car.

And it should not be overlooked that in terms of brute performance the '68 Corvette had no peers. For the 100 or so owners who ordered the race-ready L88 427 engine option, 60 mph was attainable in under five seconds. Adhesion in cornering was improved by the addition of seven-inch wide wheels and the debut of low-profile 70-series tires. Even with

the added rubber, the big-block Corvette was no ballet dancer. It literally pushed its way around turns.

For 1969, Chevrolet and Duntov began to address some of the glitches that appeared with the new body style, a process that would continue throughout the car's 14-year production run. The first item that was given attention was the chorus of shakes and groans that accompanied the new body style. The ladder-type frame was shored up to add rigidity. That helped, but the Corvette remained a noisy car.

To make the interior appear to have more room, a smaller steering wheel was put in, and the option of a tilt steering wheel debuted. Also, the door panels were sculpted to hollow out a few extra inches of room. Overheating remained a problem, but it was greatly reduced by the addition of shrouds around the radiator. The shrouds forced more air through the radiator, keeping the big-blocks cooler. To further enhance handling, eight-inch wheels were added and the power steering, now a necessity, was re-engineered to give better road feel.

The '69 Corvette saw the popular 265/283/327-cubic-inch V-8 grow to its final size, getting pumped to 350 cubic inches. In its base form, the 350 V-8 produced 300 horsepower. Readily available was the option of 350 horsepower.

One engine option that was offered – though for all intents and purposes it was not available to the public – in the '69 Corvette was a laboratory test of all-out V–8 power. Dubbed the ZL-1 – not to be confused with today's ZR-1 – this engine was an all-aluminium 427 V-8 with a horsepower output of about 550. Roughly as powerful and as hairy as the race-bred L-88, the ZL-1 was 100 pounds lighter.

If someone could find a Chevy dealer who knew about the order code, the all-aluminium engine was offered for a mere $3,000 over the $4,437 Vette base price – a bargain when considering the astronomical development

costs of the engine. Officially, only two were built, although the engine found its way into more than 100 Camaros.

A popular rumor is that one of the ZL-1 cars came to rest on a Chevy dealer's used car lot in El Paso, Texas in 1978. With a second gas crunch in full bloom, the dealer couldn't give away gas-guzzling Corvettes. Supposedly he was surprised when a buyer showed up, scrutinized the car's serial number, and paid the asking price of $5,500. Today, one of the original ZL-1s is worth easily $250,000.

As the 'Age of Aquarius' dawned in 1969, the Corvette was beginning to feel the political breezes that would shape its

existence for the next 10 years. Safety and pollution control were the buzz words in Washington and the gasoline pipeline was on the verge of rupturing. But before those forces would reach full-speed, the Corvette reigned as a King Kong sports car.

Consider the likely competitors for the Corvette in 1969: the Jaguar XKE, the Mercedes 280SL and the Porsche 911. All four were highly coveted cars, but the Corvette was capable of besting them in almost every test performance. At a top speed of 132 mph, a

ABOVE *There were five engine choices carried over from 1968 for 1969: this was the 435-bhp L71, which could be hotted up to become the competition spec L88.*

RIGHT *For 1969, the separate backup lights at the rear were incorporated into the inboard tail-lamps.*

300-horsepower, 350 cubic-inch Corvette was faster by far than any of the European standard bearers. The XKE, which was not ageing well, could only muster 119 mph in US trim. The Mercedes was slower still, at 114 mph, and only the 911 could come close, at 112 mph. The Jaguar and the Corvette were neck-and-neck to 60 mph, with times of about 8.0 seconds, and the Vette was much quicker than the Mercedes and 911. With a big-block under the hood, the Corvette could run away and hide from the three Europeans.

And critics of the Corvette's ability to get around corners were also surprised by the American's lateral acceleration. Only the much lighter 911 was able to achieve a higher score than the Corvette's .749g in a *Road & Track* comparison test. The topper was that the Corvette was cheaper than the XKE, SL or 911. It would take a Ferrari, Maserati or Lamborghini to beat the Corvette, and they cost more than twice as much.

So Corvette had a considerable advantage to build on when the 1970 model was introduced. Due to a prolonged strike, the 1970 Corvette debuted late in the traditional September-to-September model year. As a

CORVETTE SHOWDOWN		
	1970 CORVETTE	**1970 MERCEDES 280SL**
Price	$6,392	$7,833
Dimensions		
Wheelbase (inches)	98	94.5
Length (inches)	182.5	169.5
Weight (pounds)	3,350	2,900
Engine and Drivetrain type	Carbureted V-8	Overhead camshaft six
Displacement (c.i.)	350	170
Horsepower	350	170
Transmission	Three-speed automatic	Four-speed automatic
Performance		
0–60 mph	7.2 seconds	9.9 seconds
Top Speed	124 mph	114 mph

result, more than 38,000 1969 Corvettes were sold, compared to only 17,000 '70 models.

The 1970 Corvette continued the theme of refinement. The body side vents were altered, as was the front grille. Both adopted an egg-crate theme that would remain for three years. Greater efforts at improving quality control were also underway, though progress was slow.

In terms of performance, 1970 was a watershed year. For the first time since the Blue Flame Six, the new Corvette was less powerful than the previous year's model.

BELOW *On the 1968–69 models, the body-side tuck-under was found to be prone to stone damage, so for 1970 the back portions of each wheel opening were flared slightly. Most external changes, however, were once again only in detailing.*

Though the gas crisis was still three years away, tighter exhaust emission standards were changing America's cars. The once unbridled high-horsepower engines were hamstrung by air injection pumps and restrictive timing to get under the maximum pollution limits. Engines such as the 427, which relied on being in a very precise state of tune, were now very untractable.

BELOW *The seats for the 1970 Corvette were reshaped to give better lateral support and more headroom.*

As a stopgap measure, GM increased the overall displacement of the 427 to 454 cubic inches, but reduced the state of tune so that the bigger engine only produced 390 horsepower. The 454 Corvette was a monster of a car, but it was no L-88. The era of more-is-less and less-is-more had come to the Corvette.

But with the decline of the big-block came a welcome addition to the Corvette's small-block line-up, the LT-1. Equipped with solid lifters, this jewel of an engine set up a happy clatter while producing 370 horsepower. Capable of running at speeds nearly equal to the brawniest 427s, the LT-1 was the last grasp at all-out performances for the Corvette. But since LT-1 Corvettes .came without all the power-assist bells and whistles that many Vette buyers had come to expect, the LT-1 had limited appeal. In its solid-lifter, all-out performance incarnation, the LT-1 lasted only two years.

Performance took another big hit in 1971, when the compression ratios of all GM engines were reduced so that they could run on unleaded 91-octane gasoline. It would be another decade before engine technology game to grips with producing copious horsepower on low-octane fuel.

Also whittled down in 1971 was the lengthy engine and transmission option list that had been a hallmark of the Corvette. Manufacturers would have to get each and every engine-transmission combination smog certified through rigorous 50,000-mile tests. Such tests were expensive, and with an eye toward the profit/loss column, GM streamlined its engine offerings. While regular passenger cars were not hurt too badly by this move, special cars such as the Corvette were effectively crippled.

For 1972, only three engines were available – the base 350, the LT-1 and an emasculated 454 dubbed the LS-5. If you lived in California, which of necessity had tighter smog regulations, your Corvette engine choices were limited to the two versions of the 350-cubic-inch V-8. The LS-5 was just too dirty for polite company.

At the same time all this dismal news was coming from the engine compartment, Detroit changed the way it measured horsepower. Joining the rest of the world, Detroit would henceforth measure horsepower in 'net' figures – a figure that reflected engine power delivered at the rear wheels, not running free on a dynamometer. Numbers took a tumble. The base 350 engine rating, which two years earlier had been 300 horsepower, dropped to a mere 200.

Putting the best possible face on it, this move to smaller numbers could be viewed as an effort to give the buyer more realistic information. It could also be viewed as a way of taking the scare factor out of engine power as a way to dodge the safety lobby. But more likely it was a way to mask the real drop in power that Detroit was being forced to present.

The last area in which the federal auto regulations affected the Corvette came in 1973, when the first energy-absorbing bumper appeared. Masked by body-colored plastic, the longer front snout was mounted on two bolts that contracted in impacts of 5 mph. On the plus side, the new bumper was nicely integrated into the Corvette styling and was reminiscent of the Mako Shark show car. On the negative side, it added more weight at a time when the Corvette was losing power.

It's impossible to consider all the negative things happening to the automotive market in

BELOW *1972 was the last year for chrome front bumpers, because of the federally mandated five-mph impact rules. (It was also the last year for the removable rear window on the coupe.)*

the early 1970s – safety and smog regulations, as well as the first OPEC oil embargo – and not come away with the impression that the Corvette must have seen lean days on the sales floor.

Simply on the basis of its appeal as America's only sports car – and the outright demise of other US performance cars such as the Pontiac GTO and full-size Mustang – Corvette sales continued strong. From the strike-shortened 1970 model year through 1973, Corvette sales rose from 17,000 to more than 30,000 a year. The climb would continue throughout the '70s.

CORVETTE SHOWDOWN		
	1973 LT-1 CORVETTE	**1973 PORSCHE 911E**
Price	$7,513	$9,500
Dimensions		
Wheelbase (inches)	98	89.4
Length (inches)	184.7	168.4
Weight (pounds)	3,815	2,485
Engine and Drivetrain type	Carbureted V-8	Flat six
Displacement (c.i.)	350	143
Horsepower	250	134
Transmission	Four-speed manual	Four-speed manual
Performance		
0–60 mph	7.2 seconds	7.6 seconds
Top Speed	124 mph	135 mph

Americans had come to grips with the idea of the Corvette as a luxury two-seater with some performance pretensions. They liked the idea of a mild sports car with all the comforts of a Cadillac – power windows, door locks, air-condition, AM-FM stereo. And for all those people who sneer at such a trend as being distinctly American, it should be noted that Mercedes did much the same thing with its SL and that Jaguar deep-sixed the XKE in favor of the cruise-oriented XJ-S.

In keeping with its new imge, the effort at smoothing the Corvette ride was stepped up,

ABOVE AND LEFT *The experimental Corvette 4-rotor of 1973 lived up to its looks in terms of drag – .325 Cd. Most cars at the time were lucky to break .40.*

OPPOSITE *Corvette experimental 2-rotor, 1973; the oil crisis effectively put a stop to GM's rotary program just as it was taking off.*

as was the never-ending battle against squeaks and rattles. Great strides in both arenas were made with the introduction of radial tires and rubber mounting points for the fiberglass body.

The 1974 Corvette got a rounded soft rear end treatment to match the rubber front bumper introduced a year earlier. The big-block engine would make its swan song in '74. At just 275 horsepower, the 454 cubic-inch

difficult for some owners to accept being trounced by cars built a decade earlier. In 1975, another vestige of the Corvette's heritage went away The last Sting Ray convertible rolled off the St Louis assembly line in June. As the Corvette became a touring car, drop-top sales had slipped to just 12 per cent of production.

It almost defined logic, but Corvette sales in 1975 were above 38,000. The ever-higher

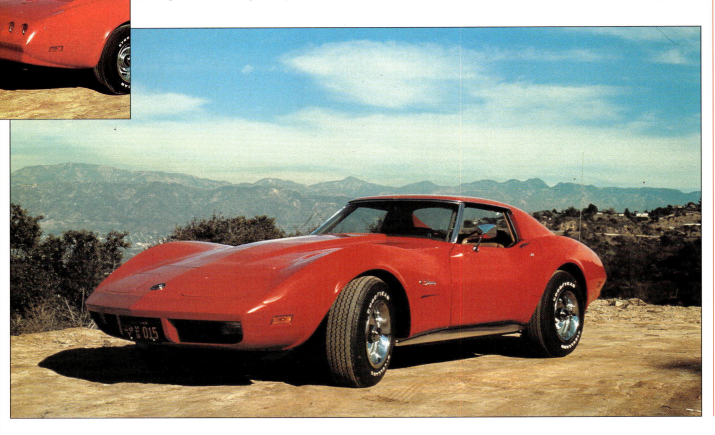

TOP AND ABOVE *1974 was the last year of the big-block engine; fewer than 10% of the 37,502 Corvettes built that year had Mark IV power.*

V-8 was a shadow of the quaking 427s of the late 1960s. Concerns about the cost of gasoline and the color of the air made the big-block a dinosaur. When the '75 model appeared, the big-block would be gone.

Although the 1975 Corvette was almost identical to the '74, the engines continued their decline in power and catalytic converters appeared on the exhaust pipes. Power was down to 165 horsepower for the base L-48 350-cubic-inch engine and the optional L-84 wasn't much better at 205 horsepower. Zero-to-60 mph times were up over eight seconds. The Corvette was still faster than most other new cars, but it was

sticker prices – now well above $7,000 – and the ever-lower performance didn't seem to bother too many people. The Vette was still the slickest-looking ride on the boulevard.

For true Corvette fans, 1975 must have seemed a bleak year indeed, for it was then that Zora Arkus-Duntov, 'the father of the Corvette,' retired. He was the man who had championed a misunderstood limited-production car in 1954 and had seen it through lean and robust times. That he was

leaving when horsepower was at an ebb seemed fitting. If Corvette lovers had gotten a peek then at what Duntov's successor, David McLellan, would develop in only nine years, their spirits would have been considerably higher.

With the arrival of the 1976 Corvette, Detroit had begun to get a handle on the pollution/gas mileage game and there were a few signs that performance was not totally dead in the Corvette. The optional L-82 engine was up to 210 horsepower and lighter aluminium wheels helped lower acceleration times. Those gains were enhanced in 1977 with sharp suspension modifications that increased cornering ability without sacrificing ride quality. Stying for the two years remained essentially unchanged and sales continued to grow, hitting 49,213.

A milestone was looming for Corvette in 1978. It had been 25 years since the Motorama car of Harley Earl went into production. Never a company to miss a promotional opportunity, GM and McLellan set about getting the Corvette gussied-up for the party.

New in '78 was a glass fastback that added tremendously to the car's cargo space.

ABOVE *By 1978, McLellan had really come into his own, offering a sleek glass fastback and squeezing more power from the trusty 350 smallblock.*

TOP *1976 saw the first Corvette produced by David R. McLellan, following Zora Arkus-Duntov's retirement. The aluminum wheels cancelled in 1973 finally made it into production.*

LEFT *The 1975 Corvette had come to terms with the demands of emissions and safety regulations and costly fuel. Power levels were at the lowest they would ever be, but the steady climb back to real performance was about to begin.*

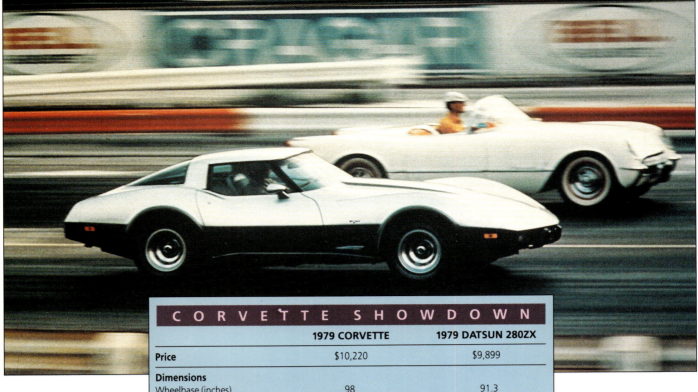

CORVETTE SHOWDOWN		
	1979 CORVETTE	**1979 DATSUN 280ZX**
Price	$10,220	$9,899
Dimensions		
Wheelbase (inches)	98	91.3
Length (inches)	185.2	174
Weight (pounds)	3,655	2,900
Engine and Drivetrain type	Carbureted V-8	Fuel-injected SOHC Six
Displacement (c.c.)	5735	2753
Horsepower	220	132
Transmission	Three-speed automatic	Three-speed automatic
Performance		
0–60 mph	6.6 seconds	10.2 seconds
Top Speed	130 mph	125 mph

BELOW 25th anniversary badging for 1978.

TOP A 1978 Corvette salutes its venerable 1953 predecessor.

BELOW In 1979, power crept up again, with the L-82 picking up another five horses for a (still fairly modest) 225 total.

The interior also got a new instrument and door panels. Underhood performance was improved slightly again on the optional L-82 engine, which reached 220 horsepower. But California – an important market for the Vette – was cut out of the extra ponies because of stricter exhaust emission standards.

Although all Corvettes in '78 carried Silver Anniversary logos, the cars most remembered from that year are the two-tone special editions. There is some confusion about the two anniversary packages offered that year. One was a paint-and-trim package in which a

*ABOVE The two-tone
Silver Anniversary
package for 1978: a $780
surcharge for really
standing out on the
street, $340 for wheels,
$40 for mirrors, and
$400 for paint.*

standard Vette was painted light silver on top and dark silver on the bottom. Special wheels and mirrors were included in the $780 package.

The other anniversary package was the Pace Car edition, which was patterned after the car that was used to pace the '78 Indianapolis 500. The Pace Car Corvette had every known option, plus a few that weren't available elsewhere, such as special high-backed bucket seats destined for the '78 Vette. Pace Car Vettes can be spotted by the silver-on-top, black-on-bottom scheme and the additional spoilers. A set of gaudy decals were also included.

Out of more than 46,000 Corvettes built in '78, 6,501 were Pace Car Corvettes. All sold quickly, despite the hefty $13,653 price. In fact, some entrepreneurs tried to resell the cars at huge markups. Asking prices in the Wall Street Journal hit $25,000. Though still a definite collector item, prices for a Pace Car model have since fallen to more reasonable levels.

Much of the equipment on the Pace Car model was carried over to the '79 Corvette, which remained largely unchanged. Power inched up again, with the base engine at 195 horsepower and the optional L-82 at 225. A record 49,901 Corvettes rolled out of dealer showrooms.

By the start of the 1980s, the Sting Ray was on its last legs, despite the slight uptick in power and refinement in the late '70s. For 1980, the Corvette got a more aggressive facelift, complete with a set of spoilers fore and aft. But there was little doubt that a new car was needed. As *Road & Track* put it, 'If you're a Corvette fan, exterior styling has held up over the years . . . It has evolved to the point of super swoopiness if you like it, something of a Corvette caricature if you don't.'

The 1980 Corvette ran foul of even tighter California emission standards and buyers in that state offered only a 180-horsepower 305-cubic-inch V-8. Also, Corporate Average Fuel Economy standards – in which all the cars in a manufacturer's stable must average a certain miles-per-gallon figure – forced the installation of a tall 3.07 rear gear in all Corvettes. Acceleration suffered as a result. For the first time, sales began to slip. Only 40,000 1980 models were sold and that figure remained constant for 1981.

While the new design was being readied, the considerable money spent on research and development meant that the current car had to make do in some areas. As a cost-cutting measure, the Corvette was made a single-engine car in '81, something that had not happened since 1954. The only available

C O R V E T T E S H O W D O W N		
	1980 CORVETTE	**1980 PORSCHE 928**
Price	$15,598	$37,930
Dimensions		
Wheelbase (inches)	98	98.3
Length (inches)	185.3	175.7
Weight (pounds)	3,590	3,550
Engine and Drivetrain type	Carbureted V-8	Fuel-injected V-8
Displacement (c.i.)	350	220
Horsepower	190	170
Transmission	Four-speed manual	Three-speed automatic
Performance		
0–60 mph	9.2 seconds	8.1 seconds
Top Speed	124 mph	140 mph

The 1981 model was also the last model to be built at Chevrolet's St Louis assembly line. Too outmoded for the high-tech demands of automotive production in the '80s, the St Louis facility was shut down and Corvette production was moved to a new, modern plant in Bowling Green, Kentucky. The move was the first visible signal that a new day was coming for the Corvette.

Last of the venerable Sting Rays was the 1982 model, which also had a hint of the type of technology that would appear on the new Corvette. For the first time since 1965, fuel

ABOVE *The 1980 experimental Turbo II Corvette; prototype experiments with turbocharging, mid-engine, and Wankel rotor designs were a constant feature of Corvette development.*

RIGHT *The 1980 Corvette was about 250 pounds lighter than the 1979 model.*

engine was a 190-horsepower 350-cubic-inch V-8 dubbed the L-81.

There was a preview of what was to come on the next-generation Vette, however. The L-81's exhaust was kept clean through the use of a black box computer. The use of such technology would make possible the coming performance breakthroughs. Another innovation was the use of a fiberglass rear spring similar to the one that would be the basis of the all-new Corvette.

injection reappeared on a Corvette engine. But this 200-horsepower fuel-injected engine, called the L-83, had virtually nothing in common with the Rochester FI engines. Called Cross-Fire Injection, the new 350-cubic-inch V-8 used a computer and sophisticated intake runners to feed fuel to each cylinder. The computer monitored the engine's condition and could make 80 changes a second in the fuel, timing and air flow. Because of such precision, the engine's compression ratio was increased to 9.0, the first major increase since 1971.

Also new for '82 was a four-speed automatic transmission that incorporated an overdrive gear for better fuel economy. The manual transmission was not available in '82, but by then more than 80 per cent of all Corvettes were automatics.

Since there was a new Corvette on the horizon – it would not debut until mid 1983 as

an '84 model – the '82 Corvette's exterior was virtually unchanged from the '81. But for those who wanted to remember the Mitchell/Shinoda/Schinella design fondly, there was a big-ticket Collector's Edition Corvette offered at $22,538. It was primarily distinguished by a pearl-silver paint job, a dark silver gradient stripe on the side and hood, mirrored T-tops and a lift-up glass hatch. Although only 25,407 '82 Corvettes were sold, 6,759 were the collector model. It was a classy end for a truly spectacular design.

Looking back on the 14-year run of the Sting Ray design, Schinella says that no one knew in '68 that the shape would become such a classic. 'No one ever knows when they are creating a classic,' Schinella points out today. 'But one thing you do know, if you're doing something that's hot, doing something that's creative, something that you like and feel good about, is that in almost every case it will turn out to be a helluva car.

'The Corvette was done with tender loving care by a small team dedicated to doing a hot car. Bill Mitchell was a fearless leader who believed in it and was a good coach. He had that overview of the big picture. He knew where that car ought to be,' explains Shinella. 'We knew that we could produce the fastest, best-built car for the money in the industry – and we still do. The Corvette is a shining example of that. There may be things you can pick up – you can pick on most anything – but the biggest bang for the buck comes from the Corvette.'

ABOVE AND RIGHT *1982, TBI Cross fire Injection from the new assembly plant at Bowling Green, Kentucky.*

BELOW *The 1982 Collector Edition, with its unique opening hatch built into the old style body; at $22,538, it was the first Corvette to break the $20,000 price barrier.*

CORVETTES THAT NEVER WERE

The designing of automobiles is probably seven parts inspiration and three parts practicality. It is not an exaggeration to liken the creation of a new car to painting a portrait or crafting a sculpture. In fact, the comparison to sculpting is very apt, since at some stage most new car body designs are expressed in full-size clay models.

At most major automobile companies, and at General Motors in particular, literally hundreds of creative minds are employed with almost the sole task of developing rolling sculptures. Engineers produce the wizardry to move these sculptures and body designers wrap those components in pleasing shapes.

Sometimes these creations are very mainstream, destined to be a new four-door family sedan or a basic econobox city vehicle. In those cases, the creative mix probably tilts more in favor of the practical than the inspirational. At other times, the creative taps are turned wide open and designers and the development engineers are set loose to answer the question, 'What if . . . ?' The resulting car is often called a 'design study,' or a 'dream car,' or 'an engineering test bed.' The end product is almost always exciting, thought-provoking and stunning.

Given the Corvette's roots as just such a 'dream car' from GM's 1953 Motorama,

It is always difficult to assess the impact of the more extraordinary styling exercises and prototypes on the final production cars, such as the Astro I (right) and the bizarre Astro III (above). In these two cases, publicity is all that was really generated.

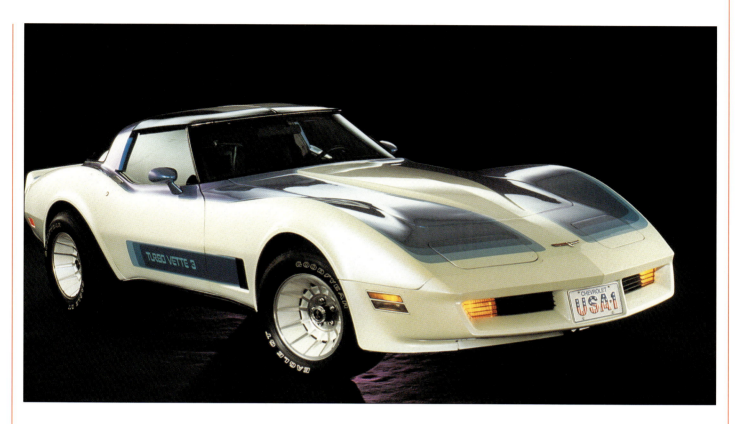

America's sports car has been the springboard for a significant number of wild spinoffs. The exact number of Corvette-based design specials is unknown For a host of reasons – corporate secrecy, product liability and haphazard record-keeping among them – GM has no portfolio of all the Corvette designs progressed beyond sketches. However, there's no doubt that the gnomes at the GM Styling Studio turned out some stunning cars with the

ABOVE *A more realistic prototype from the early 1980s, which no doubt helped to form the later turbocharged 'Vettes: the Turbo III.*

Corvette logo. Many still exist and there's photographic evidence of the ones that went to the crusher after their moment in the spotlight.

After creating the Corvette, designers wasted no time playing with the concept. Less than a year after the Corvette went into production, an entire line-up of 'What if?' Corvettes appeared at the 1954 Motorama show in New York. Barely 300 Corvettes had found their way into private hands and already the Styling Studio designers were stretching their talents.

In addition to the standard roadster, the Styling Studio whipped up a hardtop Corvette and two wilder models – a fastback dubbed the Corvair and a little station wagon called the Nomad. It is hard to imagine that at the time these designs were little more than whimsical efforts where the Corvette was concerned. There was no logical reason to suppose that the buying public would support a four-model Corvette line, since the base car was not exactly setting sales records.

Yet eventually the concepts were put to use. The hardtop was offered as a Corvette option in 1956, though it was removable, not fixed as in the Motorama car. The fastback design eventually became popular on other cars and starting in 1978 the Corvette adopted the theme. The Motorama fastback's name – Corvair – was also put to use several years later on Chevy's rear-engine economy car.

The Corvette Nomad wagon was wholly impractical for a sports car, but the theme and name were used in a full-size Chevrolet model based on its Bel Air sedan.

The cars that Chevrolet created in its first aborted attempt to establish the Corvette as a race car were styling and engineering exercises that had only superficial ties to the production cars. In both the SS Corvette – the ill-fated Sebring race car – and the several SR-2 race cars that were built by GM Styling, there are strong styling links to the D-Type Jaguar. It was no secret that the Jaguar was considered an ideal that GM should emulate. At one time, there was an oddball plan afoot to put a Chevy V-8 and a modified body together with a D-Type chassis and take that car racing. Fortunately, that idea quickly expired, but the D-Type silhouette is easily seen in the SS and SR-2 Corvettes.

RIGHT *Corvette XP showcar, displaying the flying buttresses and side exhaust pipes that featured in the 1968 update.*

BELOW *Cerv II, an engineering test bed from 1963.*

As with the original Corvette, the Vette spinoffs, as well as the SS and SR-2 race cars, were created under the influence of Harley Earl, GM's vice president in the mid-1950s and head of the styling division. Earl loved show cars and he devoted millions of dollars to their creation.

The man who inherited Earl's power and love of show cars was William L Mitchell. Where Earl's designs were at times almost art deco, Mitchell's ideas were pointed toward the skies. Space-age themes were prevalent in the show cars he created.

One of the first show cars that Mitchell had considerable influence over was the XP-700. The design featured an oval-nose front end and pronounced quad headlights. The cockpit was covered by a twin-bubble top that was long on glass. Side exhaust pipes were present and there were vents and ducts everywhere. From the front, the XP-700 looked like a car from a Buck Rogers space opera. At the back, however, was a rear end design that would find its way into production in 1961 as the first signal of the Sting Ray that was to come.

The rest of the production Sting Ray came from Mitchell's Sting Ray race car. Its design was so exciting and timeless that after it was retired from C-Production racing it too joined the show car circuit as the Shark and, later, as the Mako Shark I. With gill-like vents cut into the nose and its almost rapier side profile, the car indeed looked like a shark. Mitchell was fascinated by fish-inspired designs in his show cars. The Mako Shark II and the Manta Ray Corvettes were the basis for the 1968 and subsequent Corvettes.

Although a lot of the design cues of these show cars made it into production, many of them were too complex or impractical for street use. One Corvette show car, the Mulsanne, used a periscope type device mounted on the roof as an alternative to a low-tech rear-view mirror. Another Corvette styling exercise from the 1960s was the Astro Vette, an open car with an intregral roll bar, sharply honed front and rear styling and full fender skirts at the rear.

LEFT *CERV I (Corvette Experimental Research Vehicle), built in 1959, was a completely race-worthy vehicle that was never allowed to compete. Duntov built it ostensibly as a research tool, but all he ever really learned from it was how to build racing cars.*

BELOW AND OPPOSITE *Details of CERV II (1963); the real motivation behind the creation of both CERV I and CERV II is obscure, but looking at these shots it's difficult not to believe Duntov's assertion that CERV II was the prototype of a factory race car.*

Mitchell once said that the purpose of these show cars was to plumb the tastes of the car-buying public. Instead of the computer-driven, demographic-oriented buyers surveys of today, some decisions about designs and new cars were made by asking people attending car shows what they thought of a particular model.

As those days of seat-of-the-pants decision-making gave way to committees and polls, the value of prototype cars changed, particularly where the Corvette was concerned. They became more testbeds for different engineering designs or drivetrain variations. Two of the earliest Corvettes that fall into this category are the CERV cars. Using the acronym for Corvette Experimental Research Vehicle, these were the creations of Zora Arkus-Duntov, the Corvette's chief engineer.

Duntov wanted to get into out-and-out racing so badly it was almost an obsession. He was almost constantly involved in covert efforts to get the Corvette name on the race track in big-league fashion. The CERV program was one of his most ambitious efforts. CERV I was built in 1959, with CERV II following in 1963. Unlike many prototypes, the CERV Corvettes were obviously not designed as models for street cars.

CERV I was an open-wheeled, rear-engined single-seat car that looked very much as if it was built for Indianapolis. It was powered by an all-aluminum 377-cubic-inch V-8, which connected to a four-speed transmission. Corvette folklore says that CERV I was clocked at speeds in excess of 200 mph at GM's Milford proving ground, far faster than the Indianapolis-type cars of its day.

CERV II looked like a candidate for the 1960s Can-Am races. A full-fendered car, it too was a rear-engine design, but it was in many ways more exotic than CERV I. The engine was a monster-like all-aluminum 427 that drove all four wheels. Mounted in line, the 427 powered transaxles both fore and aft. The transmission was an automatic with high and low settings. There was no reverse. CERV II

was reportedly capable of reaching 60 mph in under three seconds.

By its design and performance, it's not too great a leap to see a link between CERV II and the awesome automatic-transmission Chevy Chaparral cars raced in the mid 1960s by Texan Jim Hill in the Can-Am series.

Chevrolet now says the cars were nothing more than engineering test beds, where various engine, transmission and suspension ideas could be tried. Duntov and others say that the cars were meant to be factory race cars, but prevailing corporate winds snuffed that idea. Duntov was so deeply committed to the CERV cars that he bucked corporate policy and refused to dismantle the cars when their usefulness ended. Duntov's single-minded effort helped propel the CERV cars into a prominent spot in recent Corvette history.

When the CERV program was ended in the late 1960s, Duntov argued with corporate executives that CERV I and CERV II were so significant that they should be spared the crusher. A popular story is that Duntov at one time kept the cars in his own garage until he could assure their future. He was eventually successful in getting a pardon for the CERV cars in 1972 on the condition they be donated to the Briggs Cunningham Musuem in Costa Mesa, California.

When Cunningham, a famous racer in the 1950s who competed at Le Mans in his own cars and later in Corvettes, took possession of the cars, he had them titled in California in his name. Affixed to the two cars were small plaques that read, 'For Educational Purposes Only.' The cars sat in the museum for nearly 14 years, oddities in a collection that included the white-and-blue cars that Cunningham raced in his career and an outlandishly huge Bugatti Royale, one of the most valuable cars in the world.

While the cars were in Cunningham's museum, General Motors appeared to have forgotten about them. Cunningham closed the museum in 1986, and the collection was sold to Miles Collier Jr, of Naples, Florida, who in

turn sold off some of the cars. He reached an agreement in September 1987 to sell the CERV cars to a minnetonka, Minneapolis, businessman, Steve Hendrickson, and his partner, Kerrie D James of Houston, for $300,000.

The sale of the CERV cars to Collier and then to Hendrickson apparently went unnoticed by General Motors. But when Hendrickson decided to put CERV I up for

The 1968 experimental Astro Vette, with integral roll bar and full-fender skirts.

have crossed the auction block, GM persuaded a judge to halt the sale. Hendrickson was totally bewildered at being hauled into court by General Motors. 'I was unaware of any problem until a GM attorney called me and asked how I acquired the cars,' Hendrickson says. 'I assured him that all was in order. I have the pink slip in Briggs Cunningham's name and it's all properly signed off.'

Chief Chevrolet spokesman Ralph Kramer says that there was evidence to suggest that the cars were never intended to fall into private hands. He pointed out the plaques saying the cars were for 'educational purposes,' and said there were various memos and conversations that supported GM's stand.

Kramer says GM had two concerns over the sale of the CERV cars. One involved the possibility that GM could be held liable if someone was hurt while driving the cars. The other involved the real possibility that the cars would be bought at auction by a foreign buyer. 'We just didn't want to see this piece of Chevrolet history be shipped out of the country,' Kramer says.

Hendrickson claims he tried to oblige GM by offering to sell the cars to them – at market value. Kramer says GM offered to buy the cars for what Hendrickson paid for them – but he admits that price was below what the cars might be worth to a collector. Possession – and a clear title – eventually proved to be $10/_{10}$ths of the law. GM dropped its action against Hendrickson and he was then freed to try to sell the cars. As of the writing of this book, they were still for sale at a price of about $1 million each. Regardless of where the CERV cars go from here, it's likely that they will continue to be two of the most unusual and controversial cars in Corvette history.

The mess that GM found itself in over the CERV cars reinforced the policy of not letting its show or prototypes cars out of its control. Still, slip-ups happen and there is at least one other Corvette prototype that escaped to see the open highway.

In 1964, a rear-engined Corvette prototype called XP-819 was built by Chevy engineer

sale at an auction in August of 1988, GM finally took action. Duntov read an article about the pending sale of CERV I, and quickly contacted General Motors president Robert Stempel and told him that the sale of CERV I should be stopped. They should not wind up as merchandise in the public marketplace.

Stempel apparently agreed, and the weight of GM's legal resources landed on Hendrickson. Just hours before CERV I was to

Frank Winchell and designed by Larry Shinoda, who also did the work on the Mako Shark II. XP-819 was a coupe that was powered by a 327-cubic-inch V-8 mounted at the very rear of the car. The V-8 fed its power to the rear wheels through a Pontiac Tempest transaxle. The car also featured a clamshell hood and a removable roof panel similar to today's Corvette.

ABOVE AND OPPOSITE PAGE Flirting with the mid-engined concept: XP-880, called the Astro II, was produced in 1968. The V-8 was mounted in a straight line.

The XP-819 was an interesting concept, but with that hunk of iron positioned out back, it was a foul-handling car. The project was terminated and the car was earmarked for the crusher. In an uncharacteristic GM effort to be frugal, XP-819 was sent to Chevy racer Smokey Yunick in Daytona, Florida, with orders that the engine and other parts be

ABOVE XP-882, first shown in 1970, another midships design, this time lighter, and with the engine mounted transversely behind the passenger compartment.

scavenged and the remainder of the car destroyed. Yunick did remove the drivetrain, and he dismantled the car, cutting the frame in half. Never one to throw anything away, Yunick put the body and both frame pieces in an unused corner of his shop.

In 1976, Yunick did some house cleaning and held a super garage sale. A Kansas City Corvette collector, Dick Walker, came to the sale and discovered the disjointed XP-819. Along with a partner, Steve Tate, Walker convinced Yunick to sell what remained of XP-819. Walker then had the car put back together. He had all of the custom parts, and the missing parts were regular production items. Today the car is owned by a Florida collector. XP-819 is also significant in that it represents one of the many efforts to try to build a Corvette in a configuration other than the traditional front-engine, rear-drive design.

As long ago as the late 1950s, GM's engineers and designers were attempting to build a mid-engine exotic Corvette. Some of the efforts got no further than the drawing board of some stylist, while others became working prototypes that nearly made production. The first was a Corvette project called the Q model.

Although there has been a lot of hype surrounding the Q car, it was simply an

outgrowth of the rear-engine Corvair design. Integral to the Corvair was an all-new transaxle that used both automatic and manual gearboxes. As applied in the Corvair, the transaxle was used with economy of fuel and space in mind. When this new transaxle was being designed in the late 1950s, the people over at Corvette, most notably Duntov, saw this as an opportunity to make the Corvette more 'European' in nature – lighter, smaller and more nimble.

Aiming toward a simultaneous introduction with the Corvair in 1960, Duntov and others worked up a prototype that used body work similar to what would become the 1963 Sting Ray. The car boasted dry-sump oiling, fully independent suspension and a unit body design. But as would be the case throughout the Corvette's history, the money

people could not be convinced to finance the considerable expense of such a car. By 1960, the Corvette was just beginning to top 10,000 in sales, and there was doubt that such a low-volume car could quickly recoup massive production costs. So the Q car was abandoned, much to Duntov's disappointment.

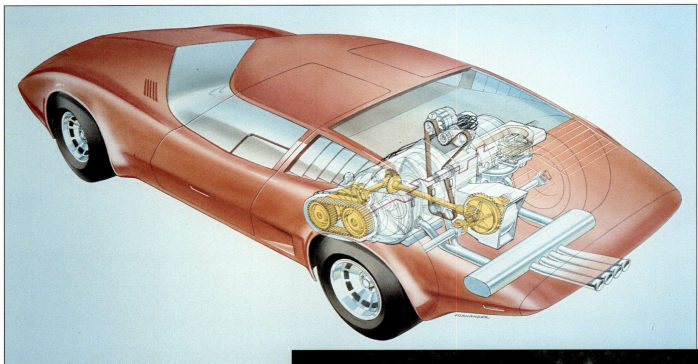

Other efforts at radical new Corvettes appeared on a regular basis. But none of them received the attention that the midships designs did in the late 1960s and early 1970s.

Of the several cars that were heavily touted as midships Corvettes destined for production, the most prominent surfaced in 1969. Code named XP-882, this midships design would go through several incarnations.

It started life as a midships V-8 design that used the transaxle from the Oldsmobile Toronado. Displayed for the public at the New York Auto Show in April, 1970, XP-882 was a very slippery design that would have been a sharp departure for the Corvette. With a wheelbase of 95.5 inches, an overall length of 174.5 inches, and a height of just 42.5 inches, XP-882 would have been shorter and lower by a considerable amount than the production Sting Ray.

Power would have come from both small-block and big-block V-8s mounted transversely behind the passenger compartment. This differed from a 1968 mid-engine show car, the XP-880, which was called Astro II and mounted the V-8 in a straight line. XP-882 was much more sophisticated, with

aluminium disc brakes and new independent suspension layouts front and rear. Overall weight was estimated at about 2,600 pounds.

The automotive press went wild over the concept and, probably egged on by Duntov and others, made grand pronouncements about how this exotic car was going to be the new Corvette no later than 1972 or 1973. That was a myopic view at best. It overlooked the realities of the car business in the early 1970s. Detroit was spending hundreds of millions of dollars trying to meet new engine emission standards and government-imposed safety standards. The Corvette, while an important car to GM, was selling like hotcakes in its current form. Why spend what would have undoubtedly been a fortune to develop a

The Corvette 4-rotor, the Aerovette, was produced by Mitchell and was a version of the XP-882 employing two rotor Wankels grafted together.

radical new car that would probably only sell as well as the current model? So 1972, and then 1973, came to pass without a mid-engine Corvette.

XP-882 probably would have faded from view if it were not for the interest of GM

President Edward Cole, a former Chevy chief engineer, in the rotary engine developed by Felix Wankel. Cole had GM pay Wankel $50 million for the rights to develop rotary-powered GM cars. At first, the Wankel engine was destined for the Vega. As an aside, Cole wanted to try out the Wankel in the XP-882 chassis.

A two-rotor version of the XP-882 was commissioned and built in 1972. Renamed the XP-987GT, it carried a body designed by Pininfarina that was distinctly European. There were no pop-up headlights and the overall design emphasized simple lines. At one point, Reynolds Aluminium even helped create a lightweight aluminium skin for the car, which bore a passing resemblance to the Porsche 904 race car.

Spurred perhaps by the slight dealt to his styling department – XP-987GT was farmed out to Pininfarina for styling – Mitchell whipped up his own rotary version of XP-882. Called the Aerovette, it featured gullwing doors and a massive manta ray rear window,

ABOVE, RIGHT AND OVERLEAF The magnificent Indy prototype was introduced in 1986. Developed in great part by Lotus, the car originally had a transverse midship version of the 2.65-liter Chevy racing engine.

complete with louvers. Power came from a four-rotor, 420-horsepower Wankel that was actually two two-rotor Wankels grafted together. Given the Aerovette's then-revolutionary drag coefficient of .325, it would have been a screamer.

The downfall of both rotary Corvettes was the 1973 OPEC oil embargo. Suddenly there were concerns about fuel consumption, and the Wankel was a thirsty little engine. Rotary Corvettes were doomed.

But the Aerovette would not die so easily. Mitchell, through almost pure dint of personal power, kept the car alive into the mid 1970s. The four-rotor Wankel was yanked out and a 400-cubic-inch small-block V-8 was put in. By 1977, Mitchell had successfully lobbied GM chairman Thomas Murphy to give a tentative go-ahead to the car. Mitchell was on the way out at GM in 1977, a casualty of retirement and changing corporate winds. The other half of the Corvette's power axis, Duntov, had retired two years earlier and his replacement, David McLellan, didn't support the Aerovette.

He wanted a new, high-tech Corvette that had its engine in front.

So the Aerovette has the distinction of being the midships design that got closest to production. But it is not the most recent mid-engine show car to carry the Corvette name. In 1986, after McLellan's new Corvette firmly set the style for Vettes in the immediate future, a fantastic mid-engine prototype appeared, called the Corvette Indy. Developed

TOP AND ABOVE CRT cockpit screens were a feature on the 1986 Corvette Indy.

under the direction of Chevrolet Chief Engineer Don Runkle, the Corvette Indy has not been touted as a production-bound vehicle.

Based around the 2.65-liter double overhead camshaft Chevy-Ilmor racing V-8 that had dominated the Indianapolis 500, the Corvette Indy is tantalizing. It looks somewhat like an elongated teardrop, with a shovel nose and a wide rear deck, and is dominated by a

ABOVE AND BELOW
Four-wheel-drive, four-wheel-steering, active suspension, and a shape to make your eyes water; but as yet, despite numerous rumors, no limited production run.

glass canopy that covers the passenger compartment and a segmented compartment that contains the V-8. Deep side scoops feed the engine cool air.

Power from the gasoline engine – the racing versions runs on methanol – is fed to all four wheels, which also benefit from a traction control system. Four-wheel steering, anti-lock brakes and a computerized active suspension are also on board. The interior features an electronic gas feed, electronic instrumentation and a mini television screen in the middle of the steering wheel that displays the view to the rear via a hidden camera.

Some of the Indy's features are probably engineering excess – such as the TV camera, the glass canopy and the electronic gas pedal – but the technology of the engine, four-wheel-drive, active suspension and four-wheel-steering are all likely to see production at some point.

Although the number of show Corvettes from GM has slacked off – the tighter management practices of the 1980s–90s have snuffed out the sort of freedom enjoyed by people such as Earl, Duntov and Mitchell – the Indy leaves no doubt that show cars will continue to play a big role in the development of future Corvettes.

THE CORVETTE RETURNS TO THE WINNER'S CIRCLE

The racing career of the Corvette can be neatly divided into two eras – pre-Cobra and post-Cobra.

From its introduction in 1953, until the arrival of the Sting Ray in 1963, the Corvette was on an upward learning curve. With only covert help from the factory – racing has always been a sour note at General Motors – the Corvette came to dominate its class in SCCA racing until 1963, when Carroll Shelby's Ford-AC hybrid appeared.

Some notable efforts were put forth by Don Yenko, Dick Guldstrand and even Roger Penske in Corvettes during the mid 1960s. But the spotlight shone far more brightly on the Cobras, even though they could hardly be considered production cars when compared to the Corvettes.

In essence, the Corvette took a back seat to the Cobra until 1968, when the L-88 427 Corvettes began to take hold. That five-year hiatus must have been a bitter time for Zora Arkus-Duntov, the Corvette's chief engineer and a firm proponent of factory-sponsored racing. He had to watch from the sidelines while Shelby and Ford mounted a multimillion-dollar assault on the world manufacturer's championship and won Le Mans three times along the way.

Barred from taking an above-board role in a Corvette racing program, Duntov worked to get some help to those Corvette fans who still wanted to win races. The biggest tool he could muster was the L-88 427, which was never anything but a racing engine in thin street disguise. Using aluminum cylinder heads and an 11-to-1 compression ratio, the L-88

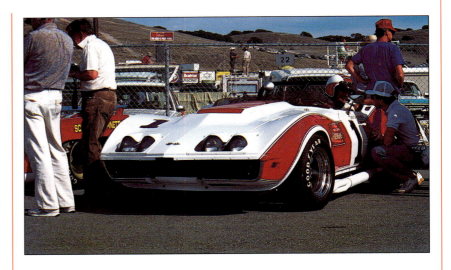

ABOVE *The Owens-Corning fiberglass car back in action at the Monterey Historic races in 1987.*

produced 550 gross horsepower box. Racers could easily coax another 50 horsepower.

When the L-88 finally came to the track, the Cobra was at its peak, though the slide down hill was a short time away. Shelby, a fierce individualist, had tired of his relationship with Ford and annoying federal regulations were up ahead. The '67 427 Cobra would be his last car. By the time Corvettes were again up to the challenge, many Cobras were worn-out race cars. It's a shame that the Cobra-Corvette battle didn't continue into the '70s, because armed with the L-88 the Corvette was a fearsome contender.

One of the first race teams to re-establish the supremacy of the Corvette was the Owens-Corning Fiberglass effort. The Owens-Corning team revolved around the efforts of Tony DeLorenzo, a publicist and son of a GM vice-president, and Jerry Thompson, a Chevrolet engineer.

DeLorenzo and Thompson started SCCA racing in Corvairs and by 1967 had a yen to

move into the big-bore machinery. Their first effort was a 1967 L-88 Corvette acquired through the financial support of a Detroit Chevy dealership. After limited success with that under-funded car, DeLorenzo and Thompson built a '68 L-88 Corvette from spare parts and raced it at Daytona in 1967. Among the drivers on the team were Peters Revson and Don Yenko.

It was after Daytona that DeLorenzo and Thompson decided they needed big-time sponsorship if they were going to become world-beaters. That sponsorship came when Dolly Cole, wife of GM president Ed Cole, put DeLorenzo together with the chairman of Owens-Corning. The deal was worth only about $12,000 to start, but that was enough to get the team going with a new car, in addition to the '67 and spare-parts '68 Corvette.

As Duntov undoubtedly intended, the new Owens-Corning car began life when DeLorenzo ordered a '68 Corvette convertible with the L-88 package. After it was delivered, DeLorenzo and Thompson went to work. The 427 was blueprinted and a special Holley 850 carburetor was attached. A roll cage and a fuel cell were added and the windshield was replaced with a cut-down plexiglass wraparound screen. With considerable help

ABOVE In 1969, Owens-Corning Corvettes took the A-production title for Chevy for the first time since 1962.

from Chevrolet engineers, the suspension bushings were replaced with heim joints and the trailing arms were modified to clear the larger tires necessary for racing.

The results of all this attention were spectacular. Starting in 1968, the new Owens-Corning car snapped off 22 consecutive A-Production wins, a Corvette win streak that remains unbroken today. In addition to its dominance of the SCCA ranks, the Owens-Corning car also appeared in FIA competition. With the car reconfigured as a hardtop, the Owens-Corning team took first in class at Watkins Glen in 1969, Sebring in 1970 and Daytona in 1970 and 1971. It set a top-speed GT class record at Sebring of 197 mph.

At the end of 1972, the Owens-Corning team disbanded, but there were plenty of other teams left to carry the Corvette to victory. Chief among them was John Greenwood, a young Detroit racer who cut his teeth on Chevy power while street drag racing on Woodward Avenue.

'I got involved in road racing about 1968, when there was so much publicity about the racing on Woodward Avenue that the police shut it down,' he says. 'My wife was coming home from the grocery store and she saw a gymkhana in a parking lot and she dared me to go do it. I took the hubcaps off an L-88 I had and ran that. It made me real nervous doing something new like that, but I made a few runs and ended up setting fastest time of the day.'

At his next gymkhana outing, Greenwood ran against some local SCCA racers who had come down from the Waterford Hills race track to see who this Greenwood kid was. Once again Greenwood posted fastest time of the day, and he was persuaded to try all-out road racing. His first experience at SCCA driver's school made him painfully aware of how different a high-speed race was from a parking lot gymkhana. 'Going through the driver's school the instructor scared me so bad I almost didn't come back the second day,' Greenwood recalls. 'He took me for a ride in my own car around a really fast, tight track. After one lap I was just about ready to beg him to stop and let me out. But after that I got the road racing in my blood.'

His first few outings in 1968 were not particular satisfying – 'I wound up being beaten by women driving Fiats' – but Greenwood spent the winter working on making his Corvette handle the rigors of road racing. 'Over the winter I kind of figured out

how to set the car up and my first race the next spring I started setting records,' Greenwood says.

By 1970, Greenwood was gaining national recognition, though all the attention was on the Owens-Corning cars. It was inevitable that Greenwood and the Owens-Corning team would meet in competition and the encounter led to Greenwood adopting his trademark red-white-and-blue stars and stripes paint scheme.

'The Owens-Corning team was the one to beat,' remembers Greenwood. 'The first place I got to run against them was at Road Atlanta, the 1970 national championships.'

Recognizing the publicity value of the heads-up confrontation – and having learned that publicity generated sponsorship dollars – Greenwood engaged in some showmanship. 'We got the car, which was white, running real good,' he says. 'We felt so good we painted it with stars and stripes for the run against the Owens-Corning car. Someone also gave me some pants decorated with stars and stripes. I said that if I won the race, I would wear those pants to the awards banquet.' Greenwood came home first and he kept his promise to

Factory-assisted Corvettes and Corvette-based competition cars are once again winning races around the world, like these GTP racers. In 1986, Corvette GTP set an IMSA record, capturing seven pole positions.

wear the outlandish pants at the awards dinner.

Aside from the notoriety Greenwood gained in beating the DeLorenzo team, he is an important link in Corvette racing history for his efforts at trying to successfully race the Corvette at Le Mans. Given all the importance the rest of the world attaches to the 24-hour race at Le Mans, it's hard for many people to understand why America's only production sports car has been a bit player there.

Simply put, General Motors has never felt the need to enhance its image by underwriting a winning effort in international competition. Racing has never been important to the top executives, despite the interest of some very talented people in the engineering department.

It is doubtful that the current Chevrolet engine used in Indianapolis-type racing would have been born were it not for the considerable influence of Roger Penske. In fact, though the engine carried the Chevrolet bow tie emblem, the Chevy-Ilmor racing engine is built in England and its ties to Detroit are tenuous. Given that GM regards winning Indianapolis as a nice fringe benefit, rather than a necessity, it's little wonder that there has been no concerted factory effort to win international racing fame for the Corvette.

There have been some notable efforts at Le Mans by private parties, who may have also had some of the famous covert help from Chevrolet engineering. In 1960, Briggs Cunningham, who tried several times to win

Le Mans in cars of his own design, entered three Corvettes in the unlimited GT class. One of the cars would finish eighth overall. Other efforts were made in the '60s, but Ford proved conclusively that it took factory backing to guarantee a winning effort at Le Mans.

Greenwood made valiant efforts at Le Mans in 1972, 1973 and again in 1976. Although not factory efforts, Greenwood says that Duntov accompanied the team to lend it moral and some technical support. That was

not enough. The stumbling point for the Corvettes was that the big-block engines were not cut out for the prolonged high speeds.

'The problem that we had with Le Mans and the Daytona and Sebring races was the long straighaways,' Greenwood explains. 'We were basically racing truck engines. The weight of the crankshaft and the other moving components was too great for reliability for prolonged high speeds on the straights. What was really happening was we were breaking crankshafts, and we were using good crankshafts.'

The Corvettes retired after leading their class. The wins each year went to the likes of Ferrari and Porsche. Back home, the Corvette was the dominant car throughout the 1970s in SCCA racing. The Corvette was A-Production

ABOVE *1988 GTP action.*

champion from 1973 through 1978, as well as B-Production winner in 1973 and 1974 and from 1976 through 1979. In Trans-Am racing, the Corvette was the outright series winner in 1975, when Greenwood took home the honors. The Vette also won the series in 1979 and 1981, competing against some heavily financed teams from Jaguar, Ford and Nissan.

As the Sting Ray Corvette reached the end of its 14-year production run, few of the newer cars found their way onto the race track. They were just too luxury oriented to be serious contenders. The Corvettes on the track were largely the Corvette shape mounted on special chassis and with power coming from an engine that could never have been legal on the street.

That outlook changed somewhat in 1984 when the current generation Corvette was introduced. A marvel of modern engineering, the new Corvette revived the concept of a sports car that could be driven to the track and then raced. It was an immediate hit in the SCCA Showroom Stock category, where it routinely trounced the Porsche 944. In fact, the Corvette won every outing in 1985 and 1986. Also, a special series, now called the Corvette Challenge, was created to showcase the racing abilities of the car. The popularity of the current car as a racer brings back memories of the late 1950s when fields of 25 to 30 Corvettes were not uncommon.

Some cutting-edge racing is also being done with the Corvette. Modified Corvettes are regular stars of IMSA's GTO class, competing against Mustangs, Nissans and Toyotas. Lessons learned about braking and suspensions have been applied to production Corvettes. The larger calipers on the '88 Corvette were first tried in GTO racing.

The closest the Corvette comes to all-out prototype racing is in IMSA's GTP category. The flag was first carried by Hendricks Racing – a longtime Chevy campaigner in NASCAR – with heavy sponsorship from GM's Goodwrench service division. Like all GTP cars, there's little resemblance to a street Corvette. About the only similarity is that the name is spelled the same. The GTP Corvette is mid-engined, uses copious amounts of Kevlar in the body, and power (in the case of the Hendricks car), came from a turbocharged V-6.

After campaigning for several seasons against the Porsche, Jaguar and Nissan teams – all of which received greater financial support from their respective manufacturers than the Corvette – the Goodwrench GTP effort folded. In its place appeared a GTP Corvette campaigned by Peerless racing. Using the same Lola chassis from Hendricks, the Peerless gets its power from a six-liter V-8. So far, the Peerless car has not enjoyed much success, with the series being dominated by the Jaguars and Nissans.

So while the Corvette has again resumed its position of dominance in production SCCA

BELOW *Corvette Challenge Series, 1988.*

racing, there's not too much chance that the Corvette will become a contender in the prototype category. And despite the introduction of the awesome ZR-1, there are no plans for a factory effort at Le Mans, according to Chevrolet. However, several private teams have said they will take ZR-1 to Le Mans.

There's little chance that the new, more sophisticated Corvettes will lead the race, given the nature of the Group C cars that dominate the field. But it is likely that a ZR-1 Corvette will some day win its class at Le Mans, fulfilling the racing promise that many believe exists in the Corvette.

Until then, Corvette fans will have to be satisfied with having their car back on top in the US production ranks.

AT LAST,
A WORLD CLASS
CORVETTE

When it came time in 1978 for GM to consider what would replace the aged Corvette Sting Ray, the American automobile industry was not in the best of shape.

The economy was still on the ragged edge, suffering from both inflation and recession. Facing the resulting lukewarm sales atmosphere, GM and the rest of the US automakers were also caught in the middle of a cut-throat battle with Europe and Japan. Japanese car makers were making deep in-

roads on the low end of the market. People were choosing Hondas and Toyotas over Chevy Vegas and Citations. At the high end, Mercedes and BMW were strangling Cadillac and Buick. So it is a fair statement that GM had a lot more to worry about than what it was going to do about a car that in its best years accounted for fewer than 50,000 in sales. If Camaro sales had slipped to that level, it would have been history.

But by the late 1970s the Corvette was important for GM in a way that it had never

ABOVE *The new-look 1984 Corvette; "A star is born" said* Motor Trend. *More aerodynamically efficient, roomier (while being smaller outside), and with subtle, flowing lines.*

ABOVE LEFT Corvette News *celebrates the first car out of Bowling Green, Kentucky. The sophisticated new plant made the redesign possible.*

LEFT *1985, and Tuned Port Injection replaces the old Cross Fire system.*

been before. Since its creation in 1953, the Corvette was marketed with little care for its relationship to the rest of the world. It was an American sports car built for Americans. Except for some die-hard sports car nuts and some car-crazy engineers on its own staff, no one at GM really cared if the Corvette compared favorably with Porsches or Jaguars. What changed that limited viewpoint was the massive invasion of the American automotive market by first the Japanese and then the Germans. Suddenly, Americans discovered cars that had door handles that didn't fall off after two years, had body panels that were aligned and well-finished, that were delivered in perfect condition by the dealer. They flocked to the better-built cars.

Detroit was slow to respond to the problem, believing, perhaps, that this buy-foreign trend was a passing fad. When the buyers stayed away, the panic buttons were pushed. New models were begun, efforts at higher quality control instituted and more attention paid to the competition.

In the Corvette, GM had a car that was still, to a large degree, in a class by itself. The only Japanese contender was the Datsun 280Z, and it was not as powerful or luxurious as the Corvette. But the future didn't look so secure. Mazda was to introduce a new rotary-engined sports car, the RX-7, and Toyota was going to take its Celica upscale with a luxurious Supra. Datsun was also going upscale with its Z car, calling the new model the 280ZX. With turbo power on tap, the ZX was a direct competitor for the outdated Sting Ray.

From Germany came a brace of new, front-engined Porches. The 924 and its much improved successor, the 944, were tough competitors for the Corvette, and the 928 was in theory the car the Corvette should have been. If GM could field a Corvette that was better than all these new contenders, it would go a long way toward patching up its shaken image as a world automotive leader.

Such was the state of the American car business when the new chief engineer for the Corvette, David R McLellan, and the head of Chevrolet's Studio Three styling department, Jerry P Palmer, began in mid-1978 to seriously create a new Corvette. The two men were the spiritual and corporate successors to the team of William L Mitchell and Zora Arkus-Duntov.

McLellan and Palmer were really standing on the ledge of a mountain when they began. Inheriting the almost suffocating legacy left by

C O R V E T T E S H O W D O W N		
	1986 CORVETTE	**1986 PORSCHE 944 TURBO**
Price	$24,403	$29,500
Dimensions		
Wheelbase (inches)	96.2	94.5
Length (inches)	176.5	168.9
Weight (pounds)	3,280	3,000
Engine and Drivetrain type	Fuel-injected V-8	Injected Turbo Four
Displacement (c.c.)	5733	2479
Horsepower	230	217
Transmission	4+3 manual	Five-speed manual
Performance		
0–60 mph	5.8 seconds	6.0 seconds
Top Speed	154 mph	155 mph

the legendary stylist Mitchell and the brilliant engineer Duntov, McLellan and Palmer knew it would be a long fall if they didn't succeed. They also knew there was a lot of mountain left to climb where the Corvette was concerned.

Despite outward appearances that McLellan and Palmer were fresh-faced

newcomers, the two men were in fact successful veterans of the world according to GM. Palmer joined the corporation's design staff in 1964 and worked on several Corvette show cars with Mitchell, as well as the facelifts of the Sting Ray in the 1970s. McLellan joined GM in 1959, working at the company's Milford Proving Ground. His first major engineering

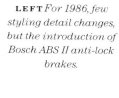

ABOVE *The return of the ragtop in 1986; because the Corvette was already a full targa, very little extra bracing was needed for the convertible.*

LEFT *For 1986, few styling detail changes, but the introduction of Bosch ABS II anti-lock brakes.*

task was the 1970 Camaro, which was so successful it quickly established McLellan's credentials. His first brush with the Corvette was in 1974, when he was named second in command to Duntov. When Duntov retired six months later, McLellan took over the top Corvette job.

Of the two men, McLellan would be the man in charge of the new Corvette. It was a position that Duntov would have envied, since the Corvette to that point had largely been design-driven. Duntov made it go, but design dictated the package. Now McLellan could make sure the mechanicals, not the styling, came first and that severe compromises wouldn't have to be made in the name of style.

The first thing that McLellan accomplished was to detail the Aerovette mid-engine design favored by Mitchell. McLellan reasoned that the mid-engine layout demanded too many compromises in terms of being user friendly. The cockpit would have to be smaller and there would be very limited luggage space. A front-engine design could be made to perform as well or better than a mid-engine car, he believed, with none of the drawbacks.

After Michell's retirement in 1977, McLellan was able to pursue his campaign without having to contend with the flamboyant Mitchell. He cited owner surveys that said the people who traditionally bought Corvettes weren't all that interested in a mid-engine car. He also had an unlikely ally in the Porsche 928, a car that he felt represented what the Corvette should be. If a car like the 928 can perform so well with a V-8 up front, then why couldn't the Corvette? Why not, indeed, was the response, and the Aerovette was vanquished to the dream car circuit.

Now working with a clean sheet of paper, McLellan and Palmer began with the premise that the Corvette should be the showcase for the best GM could offer – a premise almost identical to the first Motorama Corvette. For a corporation that had been kicked around by the competition lately, that goal for the Corvette was heartily supported in the GM front office.

Several specific areas were targeted by McLellan as major design goals. They were chassis rigidity, handling and interior space – all areas where the then-current Corvette was found lacking. For the first time, the Corvette would veer away from the construction method where the body was mounted as a separate unit on the frame. The new Corvette would use a birdcage unit structure on which the body panels would hang. This method allowed engineers to stiffen up the frame considerably without creating rattles in the body, which would now be an integral part of the chassis.

The traditional front suspension design of unequal upper and lower A-arms was retained, but instead of coil springs at each wheel, a single leaf spring ran between the lower A-arms. Normally, such an arrangement

ABOVE AND BELOW *The 1986 Indy 500 Pace Car replica; all convertibles were provided with the pace car decals, but it was up to the owner to decide whether or not to apply them.*

OPPOSITE *New wheels were designed for 1986; the Z51 package offered 17-inch wheels to clear the oversize rotors.*

would be too heavy, but the spring was made of reinforced fiberglass and weighed 50 per cent less than a steel spring. Weight was also saved on the A-arms, which were forged from aluminum. Tube shock absorbers were also used and a hefty 20mm anti-roll bar was installed.

Out back, the suspension underwent a major metamorphosis. Gone was the three-link independent suspension that was introduced in 1963. In its place was a five-link setup that used forged alloy in two trailing links, a lower lateral link and another link to keep track of toe-in. The U-jointed half-shafts and a reinforced fiberglass transverse leaf spring rounded out the suspension.

Steering would also change in the new Corvette. Since 1953, the Corvette had used a Saginaw recirculating ball type system. In the 1980s, Corvette would catch up with the rest of the world and use rack-and-pinion steering. The rack was mounted forward of the front wheels for better response and a high-effort power steering unit was attached. The steering ratio was a quick 15.5-to-1. Brakes would be vacuum-assisted discs at each corner using massive 11.5-inch rotors that were an iron-aluminium alloy.

An integral part of the Corvette's suspension would be the tires. Not since the mid-1960s had a tire manufacturer offered special shoes for the Corvette. McLellan knew that if the Corvette was to reach its handling potential, there would have to be some special rubber at each corner. Working with Goodyear, a variation of the rain tires used on Formula One race cars was developed.

The new tire would form the basis for a new lineup of Goodyear performance rubber under the name Eagle. The Corvette's tires were engineering masterpieces. The tread was cut in a V-shaped manner that gave it maximum grip when the wheel was moving in a specific direction. That meant the new tires were made especially for the dynamics of each side of the car. No longer could a Corvette owner rotate tires side to side. The new tire also used a rubber compound that was a compromise between longevity and stickiness.

In addition to their design and construction, the Corvette's new shoes – called Gatorbacks, for the design resembled alligator hide – were also huge. Using an ultra low 50 per cent aspect ratio, the P255/16 tires had an eight-inch footprint. In keeping with the performance goals of the Corvette, the new Goodyear Eagles carried a V-speed rating, meaning they were built to withstand sustained running at 130 mph.

Power for the new Corvette would come from the time-proven 350-cubic-inch small-

1987 saw slight revisions to the coupe and the convertible, most under the hood; torque was increased from 290 to 345 lbs/ft. The seats became more Porsche-like, deeper, holding the driver and passenger in position.

block V-8. If any expense was skipped on the new car, it was in the engine. For the new car's debut, the engine's power was pegged at 205 horsepower, up five from the 1982 Corvette. Offsetting the modest power increase was a drop in overall weight of 250 pounds, which was accomplished through ingenious use of aluminium, fiberglass and plastic on many subassemblies.

After a hiatus in 1982, the new Corvette would emerge again with a manual transmission. And the high-tech wizards had touched that component as well. In view of the federally mandated rules on fuel economy, the new Corvette manual transmission had to have a very flexible overdrive system. The answer was a four-speed transmission with a second set of planetary gears attached.

The added gears were positioned behind the regular gears and were controlled by the engine's computer management system. The auxiliary gears worked on the transmission's normal second, third and fourth gears – in essence providing an

overdrive for each of the top three gears. Under part throttle, the computer box would decide if an overdrive gear was called for to improve gas consumption. The step-down gear would be automatically engaged via a hydraulic clutch. Under full throttle the overdrive gears were locked out and shifts went normally up to fourth. At 110 mph, the fourth-gear overdrive kicked in.

This new gearbox, called a 4+3, was a marvel of engineering and it worked well, though many owners would complain it was unnecessarily complex. But GM was determined to avoid paying a federal gas-guzzler tax on any of its cars and the 4+3 transmission boosted mileage to acceptable minimums. For those who were befuddled by the new manual, a four-speed overdrive automatic was offered.

Throughout the development of the mechanical side of the new Corvette, Palmer was at work on the new skin. Keeping in close contact with McLellan, Palmer made sure the new Corvette was modern and complemented

LEFT *The deeper, fully adjustable seats were retained on the 1988 convertible.*

RIGHT *The larger wheel slots necessary to accommodate the rotors on this 1988 model are obvious from this angle.*

BELOW *Power increased for 1988 to 245 bhp; top speed was 155 mph.*

the new engineering. For example, the underside of the hood was designed so that it provided direct cold-air feeds to the engine.

Aside from the engineering challenges, Palmer also had the task of making sure in the end it looked like a Corvette. Just 14 months after the order for the new Corvette was approved, Palmer had come up with a body design that would pretty much stand as the production car, All that would change would be the tail lights, fender trim and the final shape of the nose.

The new design had the mandate to be aerodynamically efficient and improve driver visibility over the Sting Ray. The new design accomplished both of those goals. Using a cleaner nose and shaving off the massive fender humps of the Corvette, along with a much less cluttered rear deck, the drag coefficient dropped to 0.34. Repositioning the steering wheel and raising the cockpit platform an inch improved visibility immensely.

Overall, the new Corvette was different in every dimension from the Sting Ray. The wheelbase was shortened slightly from 98 inches to 96.2 inches. Overall length dropped

sharply by 8.8 inches, with most of that cut coming in reduced rear overhang. Height dropped slightly to 46.7 inches, while width grew to 71 inches.

The body looked sleek from all angles. The windshield was sharply raked at 64 degrees and the car's flanks were smoothed out from the tight-waisted appearance of the Sting Ray. With flared fenders covering those huge Gatorbacks, the new Corvette had a crouching appearance that exuded muscle.

But one thing the new shape wasn't was overpowering, as the Mako Sharp design had been. It was more in the vein of a European wedge shape. Mitchell would later be quoted as saying that McLellan had obviously tied the hands of the styling people. Palmer strongly

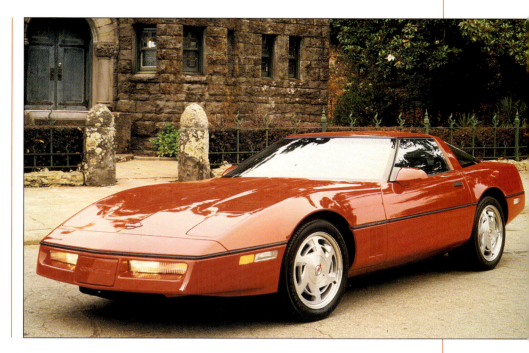

denied any such thing and he defended the new Corvette as exciting and functional in a way the Mitchell design wasn't.

A clamshell hood, long a feature on Corvette show cars, was made a reality in the new car, making servicing the engine bay very easy. Palmer and his crew were so concerned with detail on the new Corvette that they

crafted a new silver alloy air filter housing for the Cross-Fire Injection engine and detailed the rest of the compartment in black and silver, including a special battery casing. Finishing the new body was a full lift-off targa top, replacing the T-bar roof on the Sting Ray, and a clever rubber strip that encircled the car, hiding seam lines and adding a sharp design element.

If the exterior of the Corvette was criticized for being muted, the interior offered some excitement that even Mitchell would have loved. Created under the direction of Pat Furey, head of GM's interior design group, the new Corvette's dashboard was an electronic marvel. In front of the driver was a display that combined analog readouts and digital displays of all functions. The speedometer was an escalating bar graph in which green lights marched up to 85 mph. Supplementing the graph was a numerical readout of the speed, which would go all the way to the car's top speed. To the right of the speedometer was a bar graph tachometer that was also supplemented by a numerical readout.

Key readouts on oil pressure, fuel level, electrical output, water and oil temperature were shown in four digital windows at the center of the instrument pod. A dash-mounted switch controlled which functions were to be monitored. The switch also allowed the driver to select readouts of instant and average fuel economy, trip mileage and the number of miles until the fuel tank was empty.

Elsewhere, the interior was airy and comfortable. Shoulder room was increased by

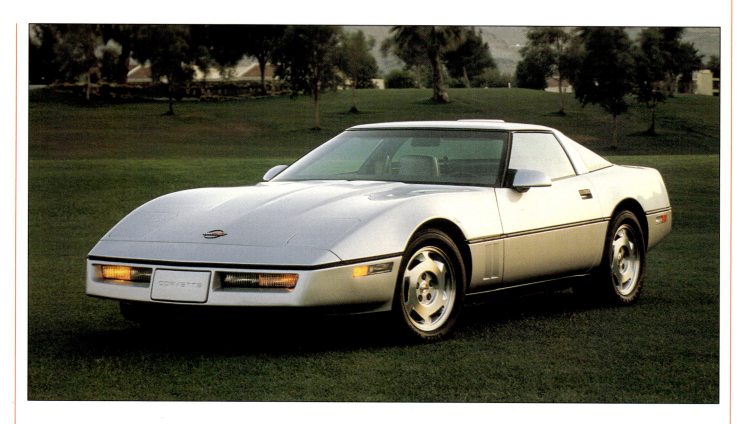

ABOVE *Aftermarket wheels were fitted to some '88s, but the original production items were handsome enough.*

FAR LEFT *The race-bred Z51 package.*

BELOW *White body-colored wheels and a black roof pillar identify the 1988 35th Anniversary model.*

6.5 inches, and behind the seats cargo space jumped nearly eight cubic feet. The two seats were deeply bucketed and were snug alongside a large center transmission console. The console contained the power seat adjustments, as well as the power windows and mirrors. If the standard seats were not up to a customer's demands, a super set of Lear-Siegler seats were optional. These seats had triple inflatable bolsters and were essentially adjustable in all directions. About the only complaint about the interior stemmed from

the wide frame sill that had to be negotiated getting in and out of the car.

In telling the story of the new Corvette, most of the focus had been on the monumental task of designing and executing the new package. The task was made even more difficult because GM was not only building a new car, it has to build a new factory to produce it.

`Since 1954, the Corvette had been built in St Louis, Missouri. By the 1980s, the St Louis plant had become too antiquated for the high-tech demands of the new Corvette. A new plant was built about 100 miles east in Bowling Green, Kentucky. The first Corvette to be produced there was the '81 model, but the facility was built for the new Corvette. It offered a much more automated assembly line and the facilities to apply better finishes to the Corvette bodies.

Spending hundreds of millions of dollars on a new assembly plant, in addition to the hundreds of millions of dollars spend on design, development and tooling were indications of the importance GM was placing on the new Corvette. It was a far cry from 1956, when a facelift for the Vette was put off

so the money could be spent on a new hood for the Chevy pick-up truck. Another indication of McLellan and GM's determination to turn out a well-finished product was the decision to go without an '83 model Corvette and introduce the new car in the spring of 1983 as a 1984 model. The extra time was well worth it.

When the automotive press got their hands on the new Corvette at a special preview in January 1983, they were ecstatic. *Car and Driver* magazine best summed it up in their March, 1983 issue: 'The new Corvette is a truly stout automobile. It is all that the fevered acolytes so desperately wanted their fiberglass fossil to be – a true-born, world class sports car.'

The race-developed GTO body could be bought through Chevy dealers as a legitimate option.

At a base price of $21,800 and performance of 140 mph top speed and zero to 60 mph time of seven seconds, the 1984 Corvette was a relative bargain. it performed on a par with cars such as the Porsche 928 and the Ferrari 308, at less than half the cost. Buyers flocked to the car, with 51,547 '84 models sold thanks to pent-up demand and the extra long sales year.

Although McLellan was all smiles over his new Corvette, there was a rough spot. In their effort to make the Corvette handle, GM's engineers created a car that was a whiz on smooth surfaces, but was a handful over the bumps and ruts of real-world highways. The base car was often buckboard rough and those buyers who ordered the optional Z-51

handling suspension – heavy-duty springs, shocks, bushings and anti-roll bars – got a car that handled like a Formula One racer, but was too skittish to comfortably dash to the grocery store.

Though stung by the criticism, McLellan and his chief tester, John Heinricy – an accomplished Corvette road racer – set out to fix the problem. When the '85 model debuted, the Corvette was an even better car. Spring rates and shock valving were changed to soften the ride. To make up for any possible loss in handling, the wheels were widened an inch to 9.5 inches at the front. Though the Corvette retained its sports car ride, passengers were no longer in danger of losing fillings from their teeth.

CORVETTE SHOWDOWN		
	1984 LT-1 CORVETTE	**1984 FERRARI 308GTB**
Price	$21,800	$53,745
Dimensions		
Wheelbase (inches)	96.2	92.1
Length (inches)	176.5	174.2
Weight (pounds)	3,200	3,440
Engine and Drivetrain type	Fuel-injected V-8	Fuel-injected DHC V-8
Displacement (c.c.)	5733	2926
Horsepower	205	230
Transmission	Four-speed automatic	Five-speed manual
Performance		
0–60 mph	7.0 seconds	6.8 seconds
Top Speed	139 mph	142 mph

And the straight-line performance was also enhanced for 1985 with the addition of Tuned Port Injection to the 350 V-8. This system replaced the Cross Fire Injection of the '84 model and increased horsepower to 230, with torque set at 330 pounds. Fitting the 350 V-8 with a computer-controlled injector at every port not only increase horsepower, but also gas mileage.

Top speed hit 150 mph and the zero-to-60 mph time dropped to 6.2 seconds. The quarter-mile could be covered in 14.6 seconds. That performance bested a Ferrari 308GTBi, which at the time cost nearly $60,000, compared to the $24,878 base price of the Corvette.

Sales of the Corvette dropped to about 39,000 a year in 1985, which reflects the leveling off of demand after the wild sales year in 1984. A sales level of 30,000–40,000 is probably normal for a car in the Corvette's price range, and yearly sales have hovered at about that mark since 1985. The theme of constant improvement in the high-tech Corvette continued in 1986, when Bosch anti-lock brakes were added to the package, as was a sophisticated anti-theft system and a less-restrictive dual exhaust system.

But the big news in 1986 was the return of the Corvette convertible. Though pronounced dead in the mid-1970s, Americans were demanding the return of the open-air car. The new Corvette ragtop picked up where the last model in 1975 left off. The top when down was still hidden underneath a pop-open body panel behind the cockpit. One person could still raise or lower the manual top in considerably less than a minute.

One way in which convertibles had changed between 1975 to 1986 was price. GM farmed out development of the Vette convertible to ASC, an aftermarket company versed in custom convertibles. The result was a $5,000 premium over the base $27,502 price of the coupe. Still, a third of all Corvettes sold in 1986 were convertibles and an unmodified yellow Corvette paced the Indianapolis 500 that year. Behind the wheel was the first man to break the sound barrier, retired Air Force General Chuck Yeager.

The convertible also helped engineers advance the effort at stiffening up the Corvette. Braces were added to the cowl and cockpit and the result was a convertible that was more solid than the coupe. The convertible modifications were added to the coupe in subsequent years. To further help the convertible avoid shakes and rattles, it got a slightly softer suspension as well, and the Z-51 race suspension option was not allowed.

In 1987, the Corvette got quicker again. Aluminum cylinder heads – touted in 1986 but delayed until 1987 – were added to the L98 350-cubic-inch V-8, as were low-friction roller lifters. Compression was raised to 9.5-to-1.

For 1988, the engine gained another five horsepower, and acceleration times dropped

to 5.3 seconds for the 60 mph dash. Top speed was up to 155 mph. Also new for 1988 were 40-series Z-rated tires – for sustained speeds above 150 mph – and 17-inch wheels. The Z-51 handling package saw the addition of 13-inch disc brakes.

OPPOSITE AND ABOVE 1989 saw little change to the standard Corvette; although a more than worthy machine, the square end cap and rounded tail-lights mark this as a base Corvette – not the ZR-1 supercar.

In 1989, several big changes loomed. One was the planned introduction of the ZR-1 Corvette, a quantum leap in performance that would put the Corvette on an equal footing with the world's supercars. Due to development delays, the ZR-1 would not appear until the 1990 model year. Other changes in 1989 involved the demise of the misunderstood 4+3 Doug Nash manual transmission in favor of a straight six-speed manual. The new transmission has been hailed as one of the smoothest ever produced, with light clutch effort and positive gear engagement. Also introduced was multichoice ride control. Available with the Z-51 suspension and the manual transmission, the Delco Bilstein Selective Ride Control allows the driver to select one of six distinct ride settings to match the demands being made on the car's suspension.

Looking back on the first five years of McLellan's Corvette, there is a pattern of constant improvement that is unlike any other

time in Corvette history. Never has GM devoted such attention to detail on the Corvette and now it has been rewarded with new-found respect for the Corvette worldwide. It is a *tour de force* automobile that is well within the financial reach of many buyers.

It would be easy for GM to continue the current Corvette trend and be satisfied. A new, cleaner instrument display was introduced for 1990 and the base V-8 was up another horsepower. A new body style is due in 1992 or 1993. But to fulfill McLellan's stated desire to make the Corvette the 'King of the Hill,' America's sports car needed to make one more leap. While the regular production Corvette compares favorably with other production sports cars, such as the Nissan 300 ZX, Porsche 944 and 928, and the Ferrari 328, the 1980s have seen the evolution of a breed of automobile called the supercar.

These supercars are very limited production items – often just a few hundred, as in the case of the Porsche 959 – and they

ABOVE *America's first supercar makes its debut: ZR-1.*

RIGHT *The new six-speed ZF gearbox for 1989.*

BELOW *The Callaway Corvette was not easy to spot: the wheels looked different, but it was the way the car receded into the distance when the lights changed that really gave it away.*

represent the pinnacle of high performance. Top speeds are a minimum of 180 mph and often hit 200 mph. Cars in this category include the Ferrari Testarossa and the Lamborghini Countach – both street-oriented cars – and the 959 and Ferrari F-40, more race-oriented cars. Honda plans to enter this rarified atmosphere soon with its mid-engined NS-X sports car.

To compete with these cars, work was begun along two different lines to provide a supercar Corvette. The first super Corvette to appear came from a US aftermarket tuner named Reeves Callaway. Starting in 1986, Callaway offered a twim turbocharger version

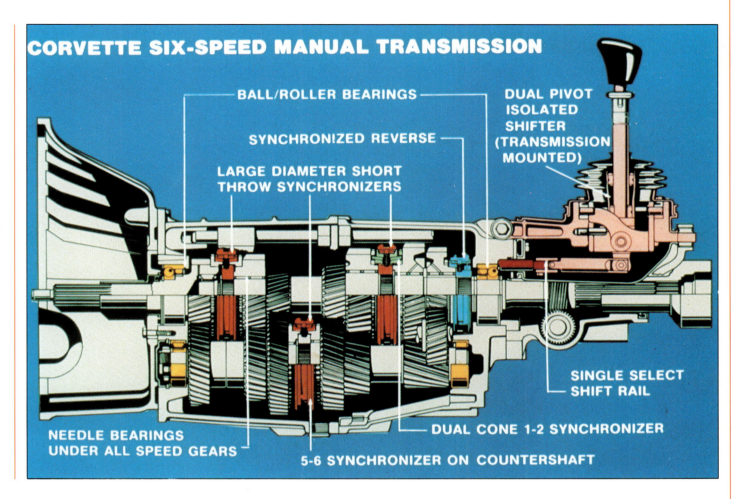

CORVETTE SIX-SPEED MANUAL TRANSMISSION

BALL/ROLLER BEARINGS

DUAL PIVOT ISOLATED SHIFTER (TRANSMISSION MOUNTED)

SYNCHRONIZED REVERSE

LARGE DIAMETER SHORT THROW SYNCHRONIZERS

SINGLE SELECT SHIFT RAIL

NEEDLE BEARINGS UNDER ALL SPEED GEARS

DUAL CONE 1-2 SYNCHRONIZER

5-6 SYNCHRONIZER ON COUNTERSHAFT

of the Corvette. Unlike other aftermarket offerings, the Callaway car was unique because it could be ordered through Chevrolet dealers. That was a strong indication of GM's desire to produce a supercar Corvette.

Callaway was the right choice for GM. An accomplished engineer, Callaway, from his base in Old Lyme, Connecticut, had built a tremendous reputation by turbocharging BMWs. Exactly who approached whom about building a turbo Vette is unclear. The resulting marriage was astounding, however, as the Callaway Twin Turbo showed the Corvette had a lot of room to grow.

Taking a stock L-98 Corvette, Callaway and company added twin intercooled turbochargers that develop 10 psi of boost. The result was an engine that cranks out 382 horsepower and has a torque punch that would flatten Mike Tyson: 562 foot-pounds at 2,500 rpm. Slipped into a stock-bodied Corvette, the Callaway engine delivered a top

speed of 187 mph. Adding new Aerobody panels Callaway began offering in 1990 pushed the terminal velocity to nearly 192 mph. The Callaway installation is essentially a hand-built engine that uses massive amounts of heat shielding to combat the high temperatures created by the turbos. It is a very tight set-up that is docile in everyday use.

Available in all states except California – smog certification there was too costly – the Callaway car was available by specifying option B2K on a Chevrolet order form at a local dealer. Of course the price of the Corvette rose by more than $26,000 as a result. About 100 of the cars are sold each year.

As hints of what else the Corvette might be capable of, Callaway also built some prototype Vettes that had astounding top speeds. His Top Gun Corvette hit 235.55 mph, and the Sledgehammer, a rebodied Corvette, reached 254.76 mph. So until the ZR-1 appeared on the horizon, Callaway held the exclusive franchise on a Twilight Zone version of the Corvette.

McLellan and his crew also looked at the option of twin turbochargers for an in-house

project, but by the spring of 1985 they decided to seek a normally aspirated engine for the then unnamed ZR-1. The design parameters for the ZR-1 were rigid – it had to have a top speed approaching 180mph and be able to out-accelerate all comers to 60 mph. Yet the ZR-1 was also required to meet fuel economy standards and be as driveable in everyday traffic as the standard Corvette.

The first big step toward accomplishing that goal came when GM acquired an interest, and then total control, of Group Lotus of Hethel, England. A manufacturer of exotic cars, Lotus was valuable to GM because it had a superb staff of engineers well versed in engine and suspension technology. Tony Rudd of Lotus met with the Corvette engineers on the possibility of Lotus developing four-valve cylinder heads for the L-98 engine. Rudd studied the problem and came away convinced the better solution was to design an all-new engine, which would be named the LT-5.

Though its displacement is the same, the LT-5 has little else in common with the standard Corvette engine. The LT-5 is an all-

aluminum V-8 that has four valves per cylinder. The valves are driven by double overhead camshafts driven by a compact roller chain. Compression is a whooping 11-to-1, and horsepower is rated at 380. Torque is a hefty 370 pounds and the engine's redline is 6200 rpm.

Dominating the LT-5 are the 16 fuel injection runners, which feed the air and fuel to the eight cylinders. The operation of the runners is controlled by a sophisticated computer that operates the unique 'valet' feature of the ZR-1.

For those times when a ZR-1 owner must turn the car over to someone else, such as a

BELOW Further delights from Reeves Callaway: the 254-mph "Sledgehammer" Corvette.

teenage offspring or a parking attendant, the extra power of the LT-5 engine can be locked out. Mounted on the console is a key-operated switch that tells the computer to cut back the power to about normal Corvette levels. That legerdemain is accomplished through manipulation of the two throttle ports in each cylinder. In normal operation, the front port in each cylinder kicks in first, with the back port coming on line at about 3,500 rpm. With the key switch turned to the valet mode, the rear ports don't come into play.

Because of the fine tolerances required in building the LT-5, engine assembly is being done under contract by Mercury Marine,

LEFT AND BELOW *The twin-turbo "Aerobody" Callaway.*

which has had a lot of experience working with aluminum powerplants. The engines are then shipped to Bowling Green, where ZR-1s are assembled alongside regular Vettes.

Its engine aside, the ZR-1 is a basic Corvette, only more so. The underpinnings of the Z-51 suspension are standard and there are massive new tires fore and aft. Up front, P275/40 ZR17 Goodyear Gatorbacks ride on 9.5-inch rims. Out back, the tires are superwide P315/35 ZR17 Gatorbacks on 11-inch rims.

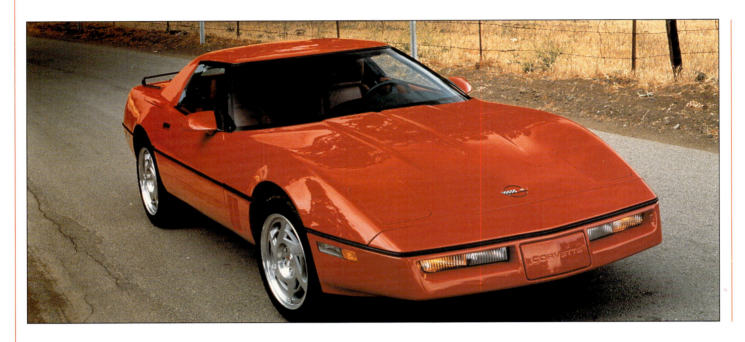

LEFT *1990 Chevrolet Corvette.*

BELOW LEFT AND BELOW RIGHT *The world-beating ZR-1.*

To clear the wide rear rubber, the ZR-1 gets a new rear design from the stock Corvette. The wide tail uses recessed tail lights and gives the overall car a very aggressive stance. Some have criticized the ZR-1 styling as being too much like the

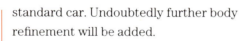

C O R V E T T E S H O W D O W N		
	1990 ZR-1 CORVETTE	**1990 FERRARI TESTAROSSA**
Price	$58,000	$180,000
Dimensions		
Wheelbase (inches)	96.2	100.4
Length (inches)	177.4	176.6
Weight (pounds)	3,530	3,660
Engine and Drivetrain type	Fuel-injected DOHC V-8	Fuel-injected DOHC 12
Displacement (c.i.)	5733	4942
Horsepower	380	380
Transmission	Six-speed manual	Five-speed manual
Performance		
0–60 mph	4.5 seconds	5.3 seconds
Top Speed	179 mph	178 mph

standard car. Undoubtedly further body refinement will be added.

Performance of the ZR-1 is all that it had been touted to be. The 60 mph mark comes up in about 4.2 seconds and there is an honest 180 mph on tap. On a ride around GM's Mesa Arizona Proving Ground with chief Corvette tester John Heinricy, the ZR-1 was shown to be an astounding handling car. It took turns

rated at 40 mph at better than 100 mph with little fuss. The 1g cornering forces were phenomenal. At more normal speeds, the ZR-1 was as docile as a standard Corvette.

With a list price of about $58,000, the ZR-1 is another Corvette bargain. Its performance is on a par with the Ferrari Testarossa, which is approaching $200,000 in price, and it exceeds the Porsche 928S4, which sells for nearly $80,000. It is likely that some of the 4,000 ZR-1 Corvettes that GM plans to build each year will find their way onto European roads, where they should acquit themselves nicely. Any doubt that GM is mindful of what Europe thinks of the Corvette was dispelled by the fact that the ZR-1's unveiling for the press took place in France.

McLellan and GM are not resting on the laurels of the ZR-1, either. More performance is available and being developed, as is computer-controlled active suspension, traction control and even better braking.

Even without these added technological attractions, the Corvette – both the base car and the ZR-1 – is a car that need make no excuses. It has handling, speed, style and grace. As the Corvette enters its fifth decade, it is just beginning to meet the hopes and dreams that helped launch a small fiberglass, six-cylinder Motorama car in 1953.

INDEX

Note:

1 All technical references are to the Corvette unless otherwise specified.

2 Page references to photographic captions are in italics, but there may be textual references on the same page.

A

Aero Coupe (1969) *63*
Aerovette 90, 94, 105
Angersbach, George 59
Arkus-Duntov, Zora 22, 49, 104
  and CERV 84–5
  and Ford Cobra 44, 47
  fuel injection 26
  and Grand Sport 45–6
  racing 23–4, 34–5, 83, 96
  retirement 73
  and Sting Ray 60–1, 63
  suspension 30, 51
Astro I *78*
Astro III *78*, 88
Astrovette (1968) 81, *84–5, 89*
Austin, Jerry 40
Automobile Manufacturers Association 39, 49

B

Bloomington Gold 8
Blue Flame Six engine *12*, 23
bodies *16* Grand Sport 46
  on SS (1957) 38
Bondurant, Bob 40, 42–4
Bowling Green, Kentucky *103*
brakes 14, 20
  1984 106
  discs (1965) 53–4
  RPO 686 (1959) 29
  on SS (1957) 38
Brown, Robert 9
Buick Riviera 58

bumper, energy-absorbing (1970) 69, 72

C

Cadaret, Bob 22
Callaway, Reeves 118–20
  Aerobody *123*
  Corvette *118*, 119–21, *122*
CERV I & II *82*, 83–5
Challenge Series (1988) *101*
Chevrolet 'Grand Sport' *45, 46, 47*
Chevy-Ilnor engine 99
Cobra 44–7, 96
  289, compared to Corvette (1964) 53
  ZO6 (1962) *44*
Cole, Dolly 97
Cole, Edward N. 11, 12, 22, 24, 38, 40, 90
collectors' cars 9, 85
Collier, Baron 48
Collier, Miles 84
convertible (1986) 116
Corvair 80, 87
  1954 *18*, 19
  1955 *19*
Corvette
  1953 *14, 15*
    compared to MG-TD 15
  1954 *15, 17, 18, 20, 21*
    compared to Jaguar XK-120 18–20
  1955 *6, 15, 18*
  1956 22, *23, 25, 34,* 35–6
    compared to Thunderbird 24
    hardtop 80
  1957 *12, 25, 26, 27,* 40
  1958 *26, 27*
  1959, compared to Mercedes 190SL 29
  1960 30
  1961 *30,* 33, 50
    compared to Healey 3000 30
  1962 *30, 32,* 33, 52
  1963 *32,* 50, *51,* 52
    compared to Jaguar XKE 52

Coupe 50
  1964 *53,* 60
    compared to Cobra 289
  1965 53–4, *57,* 60
    compared to Shelby GT 350 54
  1966 54–5, *56, 57*
  1967 57, 60, 62
  1968 *58,* 60, *61, 62,* 63
    Astrovette *84–5, 88–9*
  1968–77 *61*
  1969 63–6, *64, 65*
    Aero Coupe *63*
  1970 *66, 67,* 71
    compared to Mercedes 280SL 66
  1971 68, *79*
  1972 68, *69*
  1973 *69,* 71
    compared to Porsche 911E 71
  1974 *72*
  1975 72, *73*
  1976 *73*
  1977 73
  1978 *73, 74, 75*
    Indy Pace Car 75
  1979 *74, 75*
    compared to Datsun 280ZX 74
  1980 *75, 76*
    compared to Porsche 928 76
  1981 75–6
  1982 76, *77*
  1984 *6, 103*
    design of 105–6
  1985 *8, 103,* 115
    compared with Ferrari 308GTB 115
  1986 *7, 105, 106,* 116
    compared with Porsche 944 Turbo 104
    convertible 116
  1987 *109,* 116
  1988 *8, 9, 110, 113,* 116
  1989 *116, 120*
  1990 *118, 125*
    compared with Ferrari

Testarossa 125
  Grand Sport *44, 46–7*
  GTO body *9, 114–15*
  GTP racer (1988) *98, 99, 100,* 100–1
  Q model 86–7
  Shark 50
  SR2 *23,* 35
  SS (1956) *36*
  SS (1957) 37–8
  SS (1961) *39*
  Turbo III *79*
  XP 700 *30,* 50, 81
  XP 755 *59*
  XP 819 85–6
  XP 880 (1968) *80, 86,* 88
  XP 882 (1970) *86,* 88–9, 90
  XP 987GT 90
  XR-1 9
  Z51 (1986) *106, 113*
  ZR-1 (1989) *118, 120, 125*
  see also Sting Ray
Corvette Challenge Series (1988) *101*
Corvette Experimental Research Vehicle (CERV) 83–5
Corvette News (1957) *13, 33*
CRT cockpit screen *94*
Cumberford, Bob 7, 11, 21, 25, 35, 36, 38, 40
Cunningham, Briggs 84–5, 99

D

dashboard, 1984 112
Datsun 103
  280ZX, compared to Corvette 1979 74
Daytona Beach 23–4, 97, 100
debut (1953) 14–15
DeLorenzo, Tony 96–7
design specials 78–9
Donner, Frederic 46
drivetrain, Hotchkiss 14

E

Earl, Harley 10, 12, 21, 33
  early days at 11

launch of Corvette 14–15, 27
  racing 34–5
  retirement 30, 48
Earl, Jerry 35–7
Edelbrock, Vic 42
engines *29*
  Blue Flame Six *12,* 23
  Chevrolet V-8 (1955) 20
  Chevy-Ilnor 99
  decline in power 71–2
  427 Turbo-jet *56*
  Grand Sport 46
  L98 350 cu. in. 1987 116, 119, 121
  L-81 (1981) 76
  L-82 (1976) 73, 74
  L-83 76
  L-88 (1967) 57, 63, 64, 67, 96–7
  and low octane gasoline 68
  LT-1 (1970) 67, 68
  LT-5 121-2
  Mark IV (1966) *56,* 57
  Ramjet F1 *25*
  V-8 23
  V-8 283 cu. in. fuel injection 25–6, 29, 38
  V-8 327 cu. in. (1962) 33, 51, 52, 54, 86
  V-8 333 cu. in. (1956) 37
  V-8 350 cu. in. 109
  V-8 377 cu. in. 83
  V-8 396 cu. in. (1965) 53
  V-8 427 cu. in. (1966) 54–5, 57, 62, 64, 67, 72, 83
  V-8 454 cu. in. (LS-5) (1970) 67, 68, 72
  V-8 315 hp (1961) 30, 33
  V-8 2.65 L 1986 94–5
  V-8 fuel injected *24*
  Wankel 90
  ZL-1 (1969) 64
  ZR-1 64
exhaust
  emission standards 67, 75
  side (1965) 53

F
Fangio, Juan 38
faults, early 16
Ferrari 118, 125
  308GTB, compared with Corvette 1985 115
  GTO (1964) 61
  Testarossa, compared with Corvette 1990 125
fiberglass body (1957) *13*, 14
Fitch, John 24, 34–5, 38
Flint Assembly plant *16*
Ford GT 40 59
Ford GT-40 *47*
427 Turbo-jet engine *56*
four wheel drive 95
four-wheel drive *95*
frame, X-type 11
fuel injection, 26, 29
Fuery, Pat 112

G
Gable, Clark 10
Glass Reinforced Plastic (GRP) *see* fiberglass
Goodyear tires 106, 108, 123
Gordon, Jack 39
Grant, Jerry 43
Greenwood, John 97–9, 100
GTO body *9, 114–15*
GTP 100-1
  racer (1988) *98, 99, 100*
Guldstrand, Dick 96

H
Hall, Jim 60
Healey 3000, compared to Corvette 1961 30
Hendrickson, Steve 84–5
Henricy, John 115, 125
Hill, Jim 84
Honda 118

I
improvements, 1960 30
Indy prototype (1986) *90, 94*

J
Jaguar 35–6, 38
  XK-120, 1948 *10,* 11

1954, compared to Corvette 18–20
  XKE 65, 66, 71
  compared to Corvette (1963) 52
James, Kerrie D. 84
Jeffords, Jim 37

K
Klieber, Tony 8
Knapp Communications 9
Knudsen, Semon E. 44, 47
Kramer, Ralph 85
Krause, Billy 44
Kruse, Mitchell 9

L
L-88 engine (1967) 57, 63, 64, 67, 96–7
L-98 350 cu. in. engine (1987) 116, 119, 121
Lamborghini 118
Lapine, Tony 25
Le Mans 34, 38, 96, 99, 100–1
Le Sabre 11
Lotus 121
LT-1 engine (1970) 67, 68
LT-5 engine 121–2

M
MacDonald, David 43, 44
MacKichan, Clare 22, 38
McLellan, David 73, 90, 94, 104–6, 109, 111-12, 114–15, 118
Mako Shark
  I (1961) *58,* 81
  II (1969) *58, 59,* 60–2, 81, 86
Manta Ray (1969) *59,* 81
Mason, Rich 36
Mazda 103
Mecom, John 47
Mercedes 190SL, compared to Corvette 1959 29
Mercedes 280SC 65, 66–71
Mercedes 280SL, compared to Corvette 1970 66
MG-TD 10
  compared to Corvette (1953) 15

Mitchell, William L. (Bill) 6, 30, 74, 104
  and Aerovette 90
  background 48–9
  and coupe version (1963) 50
  head of styling 48, 49
  and show cars 81, 83
  and Sting Ray (1957) 43, 57, 58–60

Moss, Stirling 38
Motorama (GM) 11, 12, 78–9
Mott, Stan 25
Mulsanne 81

N
Nissan 118
Nomad *18,* 80

O
oil crisis (1973) 71, 90
Olley, Maurice 11, 42
Owens-Corning Corvette (1969) *96, 97*

P
Palmer, Jerry P. 104–5, 109–12
performance, 1956 23
pollution 65, 67, 71, 73
popularity of Corvette 7–8
Porsche 104, 105, 118
  911 65, 66
  911E, compared to Corvette (1973) 71
  928, compared to Corvette (1980) 76
  944 Turbo, compared with Corvette (1986) 104
prices 9, 15
  1957 27
  1960 30
  1963 52
  1964 53
  1968 63
  1969 64
  1975 73
  1978 75
  1984 114
  1985 115
Prince 7
production (1953) 15
Project opel 11, 12, 14

R
racing *9,* 34–47, 96–101
  at Daytona Beach 35
  domination of (1957–63) 40–42
  factory-sponsorship, banned 39–40, 44, 49
  GM attitude to 34, 38
  and SCCA 37, 39, 40, 49, 96–8, 100
  at Sebring 36, 38, 39, 97, 100
  SR-2 35–7
  support for 40
  TransAm 100
Ramjet F1 engine *25*
rear axle (1963) 51
Renske, Roger 96, 99
Revson, Peters 97

'Route 66' (tv program) 7, *33*
Rudd, Tony 121
Runkle, Don 94

S
safety 39, 65, 69, 71
sales
  early 16
  1954, drop in 17
  1956 25
  1957 27
  1958 27
  1962 52
  1963 52
  1964 52
  1965 54
  1966 54
  1967 57
  1968 63
  1975 72
  1976 73
  1978 75
  1980 75
  1982 77
  1984 114
  1985 115–16
SCCA racing 37, 39, 40, 49, 96–8, 100
Schinella, John 58–61
seating, 1984 113
Sebring 36, 38, 39, 97, 100
Shelby, Carroll 38, 43–4, 52, 96
Shelby GT 350, compared to Corvette (1965) 54
Shinoda, Larry 49, 59, 60, 77
Skelton, Betty 24
Sloan, Alfred P. Jr. 11
smog regulation 71
speeds
  1969 65–6
  1984 114
  1985 115
  at Daytona Beach (1956) 24
SR-2 *23, 35,* 35–7, 80–1
SS 37–8, 80–1
  1956 *36*
  1961 *39*
steering
  1968 63
  1984 106
  Saginaw 14
Stempel, Robert 85

Sting Ray *6*, 58–77, 81
  1960 *43*
  1962 *40*
  1963 *50*
  1964–6 *48*
  1966 *54–5, 56*
  1968 *58*
  design of 49, 58–9
  replacement of 102–4
  ZO6 (1963) *42*, 42–3,
    44
  styling
    1952 *11*
    1956 22–3
    1961 30
    1962 33
    1963 50–1
    1965 53
    1984 109–11
    by Mitchel 49
    of experimental cars
      78–80
    of Mako Shark II 60–1

of XP 987GT 90
suspension
  1963 51–2
  1984 106
  Grand Sport 44–6
  Z-51 114–15

T

Taruffi, Piero 38
Tate, Steve 86
Thompson, Dick 36, 39,
  40, 49
Thompson, Jerry 96–7
Thunderbird 7, 21
  1955 *20*
  compared to Corvette
    1956 24
tires, 1978 106, 108, 123
transmission
  automatic 4-speed
    (1982) 76
  4-speed (1957) 26
  manual 23

manual 4+3 (1984)
  109, 116
Powerglide automatic
  12–14, 23
3-speed Turbo
  Hydramatic 62
Turbo III *79*

V

V-8 engine *20, 23*
  283 cu. in. fuel
    injection engine 25–
    6, 29, 38
  327 cu. in. engine
    (1962) 33, 51, 52, 54
  333 cu. in. (1956) 37
  350 cu. in. engine 109
  377 cu. in. engine 83
  396 cu. in. engine
    (1965) 53
  427 cu. in. engine
    (1966) 54–5, 57, 62,
    64, 67, 72

315 hp engine (1961)
  30, 33
2.65 L 1986 engines
  94–5
fuel injected *24*

W

Wakefield, Ron 53
Walker, Dick 86
Wankel, Felix, and
  engines 90
Watkins Glen 97
Wayne, John 7
wheels,
  1968 63
  1969 64
Winchell, Frank 86

X

XP 700 *30*, 50, 81
XP 755 (1961) *59*
XP 819, Corvette 85–6

XP 880 (1968) *81, 86–7,*
  88
XP 882 (1970) *86*, 88–9,
  90
XP 987GT Corvette 90

Y

Yeager, Gen. Chuck 116
Yenko, Don 96, 97
Yunick, Smokey 86

Z

Z51 (1986) *107, 112*
ZF gearbox *119*
ZL-1 (1969) engine 64
ZO6 (Sting Ray) *42, 44*
ZR1 116, 120–3, 125
  engine 9, 64, 101, *118,*
  120–1, 124–5